Facebook Essentials

Unlocking the Power of Social Media

Kiet Huynh

Table of Contents

Introduction

1.1 Why Facebook Matters in Today's World

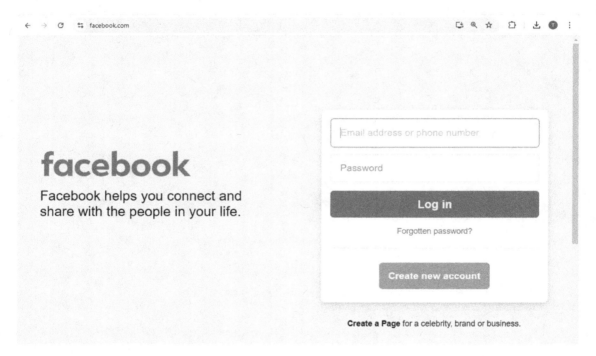

In today's interconnected world, social media platforms have revolutionized the way people communicate, share information, and connect. Among these platforms, Facebook stands out as a pioneer and a global leader, boasting billions of active users worldwide. It is not just a platform for staying in touch with family and friends; it has evolved into a multifaceted tool with profound implications for personal relationships, businesses, education, and even societal development. This chapter explores why Facebook continues to hold a pivotal role in modern society, illustrating its relevance across various aspects of life.

A Global Communication Platform

Facebook's primary mission since its inception has been to connect people. Whether it is through private messaging, public posts, or group discussions, the platform has transcended geographical barriers. With over 2.9 billion monthly active users, Facebook provides an unprecedented opportunity for global communication.

1. **Staying Connected with Loved Ones:** For individuals living far from home, Facebook serves as a bridge to maintain relationships. Video calls, photo sharing, and instant messaging allow users to remain close, no matter the distance.

2. **Cultural Exchange:** Facebook connects people from diverse cultural and social backgrounds, enabling users to learn about different traditions, festivals, and lifestyles. This fosters understanding and promotes inclusivity.

3. **Breaking News and Real-Time Updates:** Facebook has also become a hub for real-time information. People rely on it for breaking news, updates on natural disasters, and live coverage of significant events.

Empowering Businesses and Entrepreneurs

In the digital age, having a presence on Facebook is no longer optional for businesses. With its wide reach and advanced tools, the platform offers opportunities for businesses to grow, connect with customers, and drive revenue.

1. **Cost-Effective Advertising:** Facebook Ads allow businesses of all sizes to create targeted campaigns. From local shops to global enterprises, anyone can reach their desired audience by setting specific demographic and geographic filters.

2. **Building Brand Awareness:** Businesses use Facebook Pages to showcase their products, services, and values. Posting engaging content, responding to customer queries, and sharing testimonials help build credibility.

3. **E-Commerce Integration:** With the rise of online shopping, Facebook's Marketplace and Shop features have become critical tools for selling directly to consumers.

A Platform for Social Change and Advocacy

Facebook has proven to be a powerful medium for driving social change and raising awareness about critical issues. Nonprofits, activists, and individuals use the platform to amplify their voices and mobilize support.

1. **Campaigns and Fundraisers:** From environmental movements to humanitarian causes, Facebook has enabled the creation of campaigns that garner millions of supporters. The donation feature further simplifies fundraising efforts.

2. **Awareness Through Viral Content:** Viral posts, videos, and hashtags have the power to draw attention to pressing social issues. The speed at which information spreads on Facebook can inspire collective action.

3. **Community Support Groups:** Facebook Groups have become safe spaces for people to share experiences and seek advice. Whether it's a support group for mental health or a community for single parents, the platform fosters connections that make a difference.

Revolutionizing Education and Learning

Education has also benefited from Facebook's capabilities. The platform is being utilized by educators, students, and institutions to enhance learning experiences.

1. **Educational Groups and Pages:** Teachers and institutions create groups or pages to share resources, post assignments, and engage in discussions. These spaces act as virtual classrooms, breaking traditional learning barriers.

2. **Skill Development Opportunities:** Many organizations use Facebook to host webinars, workshops, and live sessions. Users can learn new skills, whether it's cooking, coding, or photography, from experts worldwide.

3. **Encouraging Collaborative Learning:** Through groups, students collaborate on projects, exchange ideas, and provide peer-to-peer support. This has become especially valuable in remote learning settings.

Facilitating Personal Growth and Expression

Facebook isn't just a tool for communication or business—it's also a platform for self-expression and personal growth. Users have the freedom to share their thoughts, showcase their talents, and explore their interests.

1. **Sharing Stories and Experiences:** Whether through posts, stories, or videos, users document their lives and milestones. This fosters a sense of belonging and connection.

2. **Discovering Communities:** From niche hobbies like birdwatching to global causes like climate activism, Facebook helps people find like-minded individuals.

3. **Mental Health Awareness:** Facebook's initiatives to promote mental health, such as connecting users to local resources or allowing them to signal when they're in distress, highlight its commitment to well-being.

The Challenges and Responsibilities of Facebook's Influence

While Facebook has undeniably transformed communication, business, and advocacy, it is not without its challenges. The platform's global reach comes with responsibilities that must be addressed.

1. **Misinformation and Fake News:** The rapid spread of false information is a critical issue that Facebook actively combats through fact-checking initiatives and user reporting tools.

2. **Privacy Concerns:** Users must be cautious about sharing personal information online. Facebook provides privacy settings to help individuals control their data.

3. **Mental Health Impacts:** Prolonged social media use can affect mental health. Facebook encourages digital well-being by providing tools to track usage and set boundaries.

Conclusion: Facebook's Role in a Connected World

In conclusion, Facebook has become an integral part of modern life. From fostering personal connections to driving business growth and promoting social change, its influence is far-reaching. However, its effectiveness depends on how individuals and organizations use it. By understanding its potential and limitations, users can unlock the power of Facebook to enhance their lives and contribute to a more connected world.

1.2 How This Book Will Help You

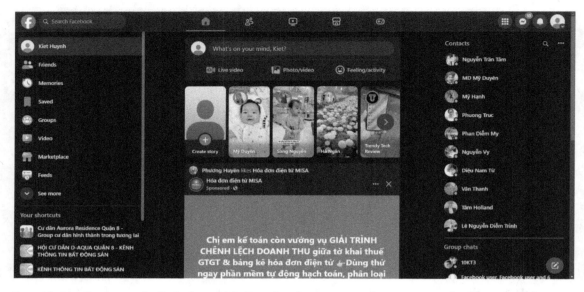

In today's fast-paced digital world, Facebook is more than just a platform for sharing photos and updates; it's a powerful tool for connection, communication, and opportunity. Whether you're a complete beginner or someone looking to optimize your use of Facebook, this book has been designed to guide you step-by-step through every essential aspect of the platform. Below are the key ways this book will empower you to unlock the full potential of Facebook:

Building Confidence with the Basics

For many users, the most daunting part of using Facebook is simply getting started. This book breaks down the process of creating an account, setting up a profile, and navigating the interface in simple, easy-to-follow steps. By the time you complete the first chapter, you will feel confident in your ability to use Facebook's essential features and personalize your profile to reflect your identity.

We cover everything from choosing a strong password to uploading your first profile picture. If you've ever been intimidated by technology, rest assured this book speaks your language, guiding you in a non-technical, approachable way.

Enhancing Your Communication Skills

Facebook isn't just a platform for connecting with friends and family; it's also a place to share ideas, join communities, and participate in conversations. This book will teach you how to use posts, comments, and messages effectively to express yourself and interact with others.

You'll learn:

- How to craft engaging posts that spark conversation.

- The etiquette of commenting and reacting to posts.

- Best practices for using Facebook Messenger to stay in touch with loved ones or collaborate with colleagues.

Strengthening Your Online Security

In a digital age where privacy concerns are ever-present, keeping your account secure is a top priority. This book dedicates an entire section to understanding and implementing Facebook's privacy and security settings. You'll discover how to:

- Set up two-factor authentication to protect your account from unauthorized access.

- Adjust your privacy settings to control who sees your content.

- Recognize and avoid common scams, phishing attempts, and fake profiles.

By following these guidelines, you'll ensure that your Facebook experience is not only enjoyable but also safe.

Helping You Build Meaningful Connections

At its core, Facebook is about connection. Whether you want to reconnect with old friends, expand your professional network, or discover like-minded communities, this book will help you navigate the process. You'll learn how to:

- Send and accept friend requests with confidence.

- Join groups that match your interests and passions.

- Follow pages and influencers to stay informed and inspired.

For those looking to use Facebook for networking or business, this book also offers tips on building a professional online presence that stands out.

Unlocking Advanced Features for Growth

Beyond its basic functions, Facebook offers a range of tools and features that can help you grow personally and professionally. This book dives into:

- Using Facebook Events to organize and attend gatherings.

- Exploring the Facebook Marketplace to buy and sell items locally.

- Creating and managing your own Facebook groups or pages.

Whether you're planning a family reunion or starting a small business, these advanced tools can be a game-changer in achieving your goals.

Addressing Common Challenges and Frustrations

Navigating a platform as large and complex as Facebook can sometimes be overwhelming. That's why this book anticipates and addresses common pain points, such as:

- Understanding changes to Facebook's layout and features.

- Managing the flow of notifications and updates.

- Dealing with negative or unwanted interactions in a constructive way.

Each chapter includes practical advice and troubleshooting tips to help you overcome these challenges with ease.

Empowering You to Use Facebook Your Way

Not everyone uses Facebook the same way, and that's the beauty of the platform. This book encourages you to customize your experience based on your unique needs and preferences. Whether you're a casual user who enjoys browsing your news feed or someone looking to actively contribute to the online community, the tools and strategies outlined in this book will help you tailor Facebook to suit your lifestyle.

Staying Updated with Facebook's Evolution

As Facebook continues to evolve with new features and updates, it's important to stay informed. This book not only covers the platform's current capabilities but also provides guidance on how to adapt to future changes. You'll learn how to:

- Explore and adopt new tools as they are introduced.

- Stay informed about updates through Facebook's Help Center.

- Participate in beta testing and early access programs to get a first look at new features.

Creating a Positive Impact with Facebook

Finally, this book emphasizes the power of Facebook as a force for good. Whether you want to support social causes, raise awareness about important issues, or simply spread positivity, you'll find actionable tips on how to make a meaningful impact through your Facebook presence.

By the time you finish reading this book, you will not only feel comfortable using Facebook but also empowered to leverage its many features to enhance your personal and professional life. From creating lasting connections to building a secure and positive online presence, this book equips you with the knowledge and skills you need to make the most of Facebook in today's interconnected world.

1.3 Overview of Facebook Features

Facebook is more than just a social networking platform—it's a powerful tool that connects billions of people worldwide, facilitates communication, and supports businesses, communities, and personal interests. To fully unlock its potential, it's essential to understand the core features that make Facebook one of the most versatile platforms available today.

The News Feed: Your Central Hub

The News Feed is the heart of Facebook, where users see posts, updates, and content shared by friends, family, groups, and pages they follow.

- **What You'll See on the News Feed**: The News Feed dynamically updates with posts that Facebook's algorithm predicts will interest you the most. These include:

  o Text posts sharing thoughts, announcements, or updates.

  o Photos and videos capturing moments or showcasing creativity.

  o Links to articles, blogs, or external content.

  o Sponsored posts or advertisements based on your interests.

- **Customizing Your News Feed**: Facebook allows users to tailor their News Feed to display relevant content by:

  o Following or unfollowing specific friends or pages.

  o Marking posts as "See First" to prioritize them.

  o Muting or hiding posts you don't want to see.

The News Feed is designed to keep you connected while ensuring the content you see aligns with your preferences.

The Profile: Your Digital Identity

Your Facebook profile serves as your digital identity, allowing others to learn about you through your shared content, interests, and activity.

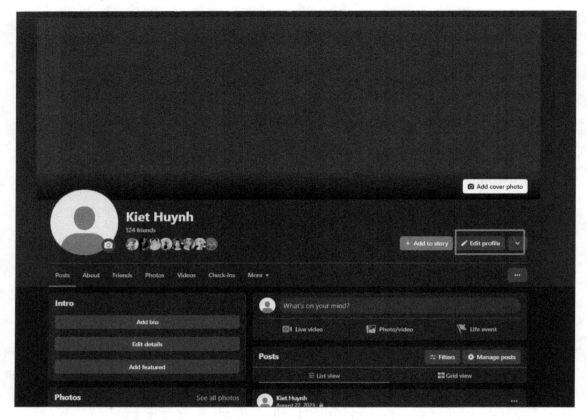

- **Key Components of a Profile**:

    o **Profile Picture and Cover Photo**: These visual elements are the first things people notice and play a big role in shaping their perception of your online persona.

    o **About Section**: This section includes personal details such as your education, work history, hometown, and relationship status.

    o **Posts**: Your timeline features content you've shared, including text, images, videos, and life events.

- **Customizing Your Profile**: Facebook allows users to control who can see their profile details through privacy settings. For example, you can choose to display certain information only to friends or keep it completely private.

- **Using Highlights**: Highlights on your profile enable you to showcase favorite memories or important milestones, making it a curated reflection of your life.

Messenger: Staying Connected

Messenger is Facebook's built-in communication tool, enabling real-time interactions through text, audio, and video.

- **Key Features of Messenger**:
    - **Text Messaging**: Send instant messages to individuals or groups.
    - **Voice and Video Calls**: Make free calls with high-quality audio and video.

- o **Stickers and Emojis**: Express yourself creatively using animated stickers and emojis.

- **Advanced Features**: Messenger goes beyond basic messaging by offering:

  - o **File Sharing**: Easily share photos, videos, documents, and links.

  - o **Polls**: Create polls to gather opinions in group chats.

  - o **Secret Conversations**: Secure messages with end-to-end encryption for added privacy.

Groups: Building Communities

Facebook Groups provide a platform for people with shared interests to come together, share ideas, and engage in discussions.

- **Joining or Creating a Group**:

  - o Groups can focus on various topics such as hobbies, support networks, professional development, or local communities.

  - o You can join public or private groups, depending on your interests and privacy preferences.

- **Engaging with Groups**:

  - o Members can participate by posting content, commenting, or reacting to others' posts.

  - o Group admins can organize events, create polls, and moderate discussions to ensure a positive experience.

- **Benefits of Groups**: Groups provide a sense of belonging and enable users to connect with like-minded individuals.

Pages: Sharing Content with the World

Pages are public profiles designed for businesses, organizations, public figures, and creators to connect with their audience.

- **Creating a Page**:

o   Anyone can create a page to represent their brand, business, or project.

o   Pages can include a description, profile picture, cover photo, and call-to-action buttons (e.g., "Contact Us" or "Shop Now").

- **Engaging with an Audience**:

    o   Post updates, share media, or run promotions to keep your audience engaged.

    o   Interact with followers through comments, reactions, and private messages.

- **Using Insights**: Facebook Pages include analytics tools, allowing admins to monitor post reach, engagement, and audience demographics.

Marketplace: Buying and Selling

The Facebook Marketplace is an online hub for buying, selling, and trading items within your local community.

- **Browsing the Marketplace**:

    o   Search for items based on categories such as electronics, furniture, or vehicles.

    o   Filter results by location, price, and condition.

- **Selling on the Marketplace**:

    o   List items by uploading photos, writing descriptions, and setting prices.

    o   Communicate with potential buyers directly through Messenger.

- **Safety Tips for Marketplace Users**:

    o   Meet in public places for transactions.

    o   Avoid sharing personal or financial information with strangers.

Events: Organizing and Attending Gatherings

Facebook Events make it easy to plan and discover gatherings, whether virtual or in-person.

- **Creating an Event**:
    - Add a title, description, date, and location for your event.
    - Set the event as public or private, depending on your audience.
- **RSVP and Attendance**:
    - Invite friends to join events and track RSVPs.
    - Attendees can engage with event hosts through discussions and updates.
- **Using Events for Businesses**:
    - Promote workshops, webinars, or sales to reach a larger audience.

Stories and Reels: Capturing Moments

Stories and Reels are Facebook's features for sharing short-lived, engaging content.

- **Stories**:
    - Photos or videos that disappear after 24 hours.
    - Use creative tools such as filters, stickers, and text to enhance your stories.
- **Reels**:
    - Short, entertaining videos with music and effects.
    - Ideal for showcasing creativity and connecting with broader audiences.

Notifications: Staying Informed

Notifications keep users updated about activity on their account, including:

- New likes, comments, or shares on your posts.
- Invitations to events or groups.
- Friend requests and messages.

Users can customize notifications to focus on what matters most.

Privacy and Security Features

Facebook offers robust tools to help users manage their privacy and secure their accounts:

- **Privacy Settings**: Control who can see your posts, profile, and personal information.

- **Blocking and Reporting**: Manage unwanted interactions by blocking or reporting accounts.

- **Activity Log**: Review and manage your past activity, including posts, reactions, and comments.

By understanding these features, users can make the most of their Facebook experience, whether for personal use, business growth, or building meaningful connections.

CHAPTER I
Getting Started with Facebook

2.1 Creating a Facebook Account

Creating a Facebook account is the first step to unlocking the powerful features of this platform. Whether you're joining Facebook to connect with friends, promote your business, or explore new interests, setting up your account properly ensures a smooth start. In this section, we will guide you through the steps required to sign up for Facebook, customize your profile, and make the most of your new account.

2.1.1 Signing Up for the First Time

Setting up a Facebook account for the first time is a straightforward process that can be completed in just a few minutes. Here's a step-by-step guide to help you get started:

Step 1: Visit the Facebook Website or Download the App

The first step is to access Facebook. You can either visit the official website at www.facebook.com on a computer or download the Facebook app from the **Apple App Store** (for iOS devices) or **Google Play Store** (for Android devices). The app offers a user-friendly interface optimized for mobile devices, while the website provides a full-featured experience on larger screens.

Key Tip:

Make sure you download the official Facebook app to avoid any fake or malicious software. Look for "Meta Platforms, Inc." as the developer name when downloading.

Step 2: Click on "Create New Account"

Once you're on the Facebook homepage or app, locate the **"Create New Account"** button. This option is prominently displayed on the login screen.

Clicking this button will open a registration form where you'll be prompted to enter basic personal information, such as:

- **First Name and Last Name**: Use your real name to make it easier for friends and family to find you.

- **Mobile Number or Email Address**: This will be used for account verification and recovery.

- **Password**: Create a strong, unique password that combines letters, numbers, and symbols.

- **Date of Birth**: This is required to verify that you meet Facebook's minimum age requirement (13 years old in most countries).

- **Gender**: Select your gender or choose a custom option if you prefer.

Privacy Note:

Your email address or phone number won't be displayed publicly unless you choose to make it visible.

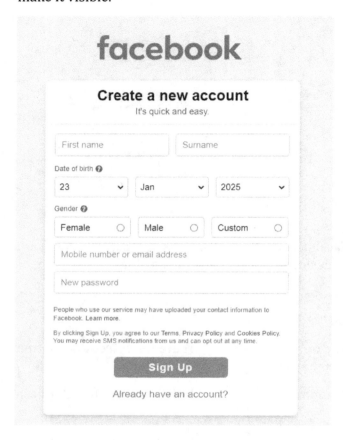

Step 3: Verify Your Information

After filling out the registration form, Facebook will send a verification code to the email address or phone number you provided.

- **If you used an email address**: Check your inbox for an email from Facebook with the subject line "Confirm Your Account." Open the email and click on the verification link or enter the code provided in the Facebook app or website.

- **If you used a phone number**: You'll receive a text message with a six-digit code. Enter this code in the appropriate field on the registration page.

Troubleshooting Tips:

- Didn't receive the code? Check your spam or junk mail folder if you used an email.

- If you used a phone number, ensure you've entered the correct country code and check for any network issues.

Step 4: Create a Strong Password

When setting your password, aim for a combination that is both secure and memorable. Avoid using obvious choices like your name, birthday, or simple patterns such as "123456." Instead, consider the following tips:

- Use at least **8-12 characters**.

- Combine **uppercase and lowercase letters**.

- Add **special characters** (e.g., @, #, $, %).

- Avoid reusing passwords from other accounts.

Example of a Strong Password:

Gr8t!Fb_User2025

Step 5: Log In to Your New Account

Once you've verified your information and set a password, you can log in to your new Facebook account. Simply enter your email address or phone number, followed by the password you created.

Step 6: Personalize Your Experience

Now that your account is active, Facebook will guide you through a few initial setup steps to personalize your experience:

Add a Profile Picture:

A profile picture helps your friends recognize you. You can either upload a photo from your device or take one directly using your phone or computer camera.

Set Up Your Cover Photo:

The cover photo is a larger image that appears at the top of your profile. This is a great opportunity to showcase your personality, interests, or creativity.

Find Friends:

Facebook will suggest people you may know based on your email contacts or phone number. You can also search for specific individuals using the search bar.

Choose Your Privacy Settings:

Facebook offers a quick privacy setup tool to help you decide who can see your posts, send you friend requests, or contact you. You can always adjust these settings later.

Common Mistakes to Avoid When Signing Up

Using an Invalid Email Address or Phone Number:

Ensure the email or phone number you provide is active and accessible, as this is essential for verifying your account and recovering it if you forget your password.

Choosing a Weak Password:

A weak password makes your account vulnerable to hacking attempts. Always prioritize security when creating a password.

Skipping Profile Setup:

While it might be tempting to skip adding a profile picture or filling out your bio, completing these steps helps you connect with others more effectively.

Tips for First-Time Users

1. **Explore the Platform**: Take some time to navigate through Facebook's features, such as the News Feed, Groups, and Marketplace.

2. **Join Interest-Based Communities**: Facebook Groups are a great way to meet like-minded people.

3. **Keep Your Profile Updated**: Regularly update your profile information to reflect changes in your life.

4. **Learn the Basics of Privacy**: Familiarize yourself with Facebook's privacy settings to control who can view your profile and posts.

By following these steps, you'll have successfully created your Facebook account and taken the first step towards unlocking the full potential of social media. Next, we'll explore how to customize your profile to make it uniquely yours!

2.1.2 Setting Up Your Profile Picture and Cover Photo

Setting up your profile picture and cover photo is an essential step in creating a personal or professional presence on Facebook. These two visual elements are the first things people notice when they visit your profile. They not only represent your identity but also help others connect with you more effectively. In this section, we'll guide you through choosing, uploading, and customizing your profile picture and cover photo to make a great first impression.

Why Your Profile Picture and Cover Photo Matter

Your profile picture is the face of your Facebook account. Whether it's a personal account, a business profile, or a community page, your profile picture should be clear, recognizable, and representative of your identity. It helps friends, family, or potential clients identify you quickly.

The cover photo, on the other hand, serves as the backdrop of your profile. It provides additional context about you or your brand. Think of it as a billboard—it's a chance to showcase your personality, interests, or message creatively. Together, your profile picture and cover photo create a cohesive visual identity that speaks volumes about who you are or what you stand for.

Choosing the Right Profile Picture

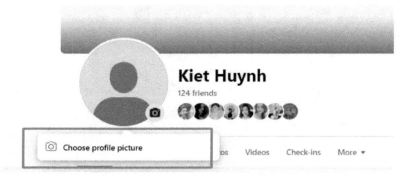

1. **For Personal Accounts**: When setting up a personal profile, your profile picture should ideally be a high-quality image of your face. Avoid overly filtered or blurry images. Ensure that your face is clearly visible, as this helps people recognize you easily. A smile or a friendly expression can also make your profile appear more approachable.

2. **For Business Accounts**: For businesses or brands, the profile picture is often the company logo. This ensures brand consistency across all platforms. Make sure the logo fits well within Facebook's circular frame, avoiding any important elements being cropped out.

3. **For Community Pages or Groups**: If you're managing a community page or group, the profile picture can be a simple symbol or icon that represents the group's purpose. Keep it clean and visually appealing.

Steps to Upload Your Profile Picture

1. **Go to Your Profile**: Once you've created your account, navigate to your profile by clicking on your name or profile picture placeholder in the top-right corner of the Facebook homepage.

2. **Click on the Profile Picture Icon**: Hover over the circular profile picture placeholder and click on the "Add Photo" or "Edit" button.

3. **Choose a Photo**: Facebook will give you two options:

   o   Upload a photo from your device.

   o   Select a photo from your existing Facebook albums.

4. **Adjust the Photo**: After selecting the image, Facebook allows you to crop, zoom, and adjust the position of the picture. Ensure your face, logo, or icon is centered and fits well within the circular frame.

5. **Save Changes**: Once satisfied, click "Save" to set your profile picture.

Best Practices for Profile Pictures

- **Use High-Resolution Images**: A blurry or pixelated image can make your profile appear unprofessional. Ensure the image has a resolution of at least 180x180 pixels (Facebook's minimum requirement).

- **Keep It Updated**: Regularly update your profile picture to keep it relevant, especially if it's a personal account and your appearance has changed.

- **Avoid Distracting Backgrounds**: A simple, uncluttered background ensures the focus remains on your face or logo.

- **Maintain Consistency Across Platforms**: For businesses, using the same profile picture on all social media platforms helps with brand recognition.

Choosing the Right Cover Photo

Your cover photo is much larger than your profile picture, making it the perfect canvas to tell your story visually. Here are some tips based on different account types:

1. **For Personal Accounts**: Use a photo that reflects your personality, hobbies, or interests. This could be a family photo, a scenic shot from a vacation, or a creative design that represents you.

2. **For Business Accounts**: A business cover photo should align with your branding. Consider using:

   o A promotional banner highlighting a product or service.

   o A team photo to showcase your company culture.

   o A graphic with your tagline or mission statement.

3. **For Community Pages or Groups**: Choose an image that resonates with the group's purpose. For example, a cooking group might feature a vibrant photo of delicious dishes.

Steps to Upload Your Cover Photo

1. **Navigate to Your Profile**: Click on your name or profile picture placeholder to access your profile page.

2. **Click on the Cover Photo Area**: Hover over the rectangular area at the top of your profile and click "Add Cover Photo" or "Edit."

3. **Upload or Select a Photo**:

   o   Upload a photo from your device.

   o   Choose from your Facebook albums.

4. **Adjust the Photo**: Use Facebook's positioning tools to move the image up or down. Make sure the most important part of the image is visible within the frame.

5. **Save Changes**: Once positioned correctly, click "Save" to set your cover photo.

Best Practices for Cover Photos

- **Use the Right Dimensions**: Facebook recommends a resolution of 851x315 pixels. Images smaller than this may appear stretched or pixelated.

- **Keep It Simple**: Avoid overly busy images that can distract viewers.

- **Stay On-Brand**: If you're representing a business or group, use colors and fonts consistent with your brand identity.

- **Test on Different Devices**: Cover photos may appear differently on desktop and mobile. Preview your image on both to ensure it looks good everywhere.

Tips for Harmonizing Your Profile Picture and Cover Photo

1. **Match the Style**: Your profile picture and cover photo should complement each other. For example, if your profile picture is a close-up headshot, consider a simple, clean background for your cover photo.

2. **Tell a Story**: Use the combination of the two images to convey a message. For example, a personal profile might feature a smiling profile picture paired with a family photo as the cover photo.

3. **Maintain Color Consistency**: Use similar tones or color schemes to create a cohesive visual identity.

Updating Your Photos Regularly

Updating your profile picture and cover photo periodically keeps your profile fresh and engaging. For personal accounts, consider changing them for special occasions or milestones. For businesses, update them to align with marketing campaigns, seasons, or promotions.

By setting up a thoughtful and visually appealing profile picture and cover photo, you create a strong first impression and establish your identity on Facebook. Whether you're connecting with friends or promoting your brand, these visual elements play a crucial role in your online presence.

2.1.3 Customizing Your Profile Information

Customizing your Facebook profile is an essential step in making your account truly your own. This section will guide you through the process of updating your profile information, ensuring it reflects your personality, preferences, and goals—whether for personal networking, professional growth, or connecting with friends and family. Here's a detailed walkthrough to help you craft an engaging and accurate profile.

Why Customizing Your Profile Information Matters

Your Facebook profile is often the first impression others have of you on social media. It serves as your personal digital identity. A well-crafted profile can:

- Help friends and acquaintances recognize you.

- Showcase your interests and achievements.

- Build trust and credibility, especially for professional or business use.

- Make it easier for people to find and connect with you.

By customizing your profile information thoughtfully, you ensure it aligns with your personal or professional goals.

Step-by-Step Guide to Customizing Your Profile Information

1. Accessing Your Profile

1. Log in to your Facebook account.

2. Click on your profile picture or name in the top navigation bar. This will take you to your profile page.

3. On your profile page, look for the "Edit Profile" button near the top of the page and click it.

2. Updating Basic Information

Basic information includes your name, contact details, and personal identifiers. Here's how to update them:

A. Name and Username

1. Click on the "Edit Profile" button.

2. Under the **"About"** section, locate the "Name" field.

3. Enter your full name as you'd like it to appear.

   o Use your real name to make it easier for friends to find you.

   o Avoid using special characters or nicknames unless they're widely recognized.

4. Add a username. This creates a unique URL for your profile (e.g., facebook.com/yourusername).

B. Contact Information

1. Navigate to the **"Contact and Basic Info"** section under the "About" tab.

2. Add or update your email address and phone number.

   o Use an email address you check regularly.

   o Add a phone number if you want friends to connect with you or for account recovery purposes.

3. Adjust the privacy settings for your contact information by clicking the audience selector (e.g., Public, Friends, Only Me).

3. Adding Work and Education Details

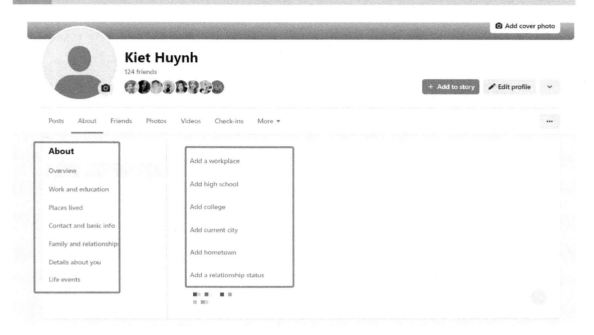

Sharing your professional and academic history helps others understand your background. It's also useful for networking.

A. Work Information

1. Go to the "Work and Education" section under "About."

2. Click **"Add a Workplace."**

3. Fill in the details:

    o Company name

    o Job title

    o Location

    o Time period

    o Description of your role and responsibilities

4. Adjust the audience settings to control who can view this information.

B. Education Information

1. In the same section, click **"Add a School."**

2. Enter the following details:

   o   School name

   o   Degree or program

   o   Field of study

   o   Dates attended

3. Optionally, include achievements or notable activities during your time at school.

---

4. Personalizing Your Bio and About Section

The bio section is a quick way to introduce yourself in a few words. It appears prominently under your profile picture.

A. Writing a Great Bio

1. Click on the **"Edit Profile"** button.

2. Look for the "Bio" field.

3. Write a concise, engaging description (maximum 101 characters).

   o   Examples:

      ▪   "Traveler | Photographer | Food Lover"

      ▪   "Marketing Specialist passionate about digital strategy"

      ▪   "Mom of two, coffee enthusiast, and bookworm"

4. Save your changes.

B. Filling Out the "About" Section

1. Click on the "About" tab.

2. Update additional fields like:

   o   Hometown

   o   Current city

   o   Relationship status

    o   Favorite quotes

    o   Other names (e.g., nicknames, maiden names)

3. Use the privacy selector to decide who can view this information.

5. Highlighting Interests and Hobbies

Your interests and hobbies can help others find common ground with you.

A. Adding Hobbies

1. Scroll down your profile page to the "Hobbies" section.

2. Click **"Edit"** and select hobbies from the list (e.g., cooking, cycling, painting).

3. If your hobby isn't listed, add a custom one.

B. Favorite Movies, TV Shows, and Music

1. Under the "About" section, find the **"Details About You"** field.

2. Add your favorite:

    o   Movies

    o   TV shows

    o   Books

    o   Music artists

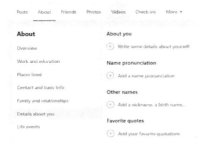

6. Curating Featured Photos

Facebook allows you to display featured photos at the top of your profile.

1. On your profile page, click **"Add Featured Photos."**

2. Select up to 9 photos that represent you.

   o Examples: Vacation pictures, family moments, achievements.

3. Rearrange them by dragging and dropping.

7. Customizing Profile Sections

Facebook lets you control which sections appear on your profile.

1. Go to the **"Customize Your Intro"** option on your profile.

2. Toggle on/off the sections you want to show or hide (e.g., Friends list, events, or groups).

Tips for an Impressive Profile

- **Use High-Quality Images**: Ensure your profile and cover photos are clear and reflect your personality.

- **Keep It Updated**: Regularly review and update your information to keep it relevant.

- **Maintain Privacy**: Always check your privacy settings to control who sees specific details.

- **Be Authentic**: Share information that genuinely represents who you are.

Common Mistakes to Avoid

1. **Oversharing**: Avoid adding sensitive information like your full address or private phone number.

2. **Inconsistent Information**: Make sure details across platforms are consistent, especially for professional networking.

3. **Using Outdated Photos**: Use recent images to ensure others recognize you.

By following these steps, you'll have a fully customized Facebook profile that's engaging, accurate, and reflective of your goals. A well-crafted profile will help you connect with friends, family, and colleagues while ensuring your online presence aligns with your intentions.

2.2 Understanding the Facebook Interface

2.2.1 Navigating the News Feed

The **News Feed** is the heart of Facebook, serving as the central hub where users can view updates, posts, and activities from their friends, groups, and pages they follow. Learning how to navigate the News Feed effectively ensures you make the most of your time on Facebook while staying connected to what matters most. Below is a detailed guide to help you master every aspect of the News Feed.

What is the News Feed?

The News Feed is the primary screen you see when you log into Facebook. It's a dynamic and personalized stream of content curated by Facebook's algorithms based on your interests, interactions, and preferences. This includes posts from friends, family, groups, pages, and advertisements tailored to you.

Key Features of the News Feed

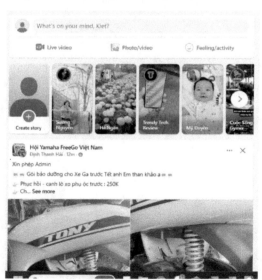

Before diving into the navigation process, let's explore the essential features and elements of the News Feed interface:

1. **Post Content**

   o Posts in your News Feed may include text, photos, videos, shared links, live videos, and more.

   o Posts often display the name and profile picture of the author, along with options to like, comment, or share the post.

2. **Stories at the Top**

   o At the very top of the News Feed, you'll see Stories. These are short-lived posts (photos or videos) that disappear after 24 hours.

3. **Reactions and Interactions**

   o Below each post, you'll find options to react (like, love, care, laugh, wow, sad, or angry), comment, and share the post.

4. **Sponsored Content**

   o Advertisements marked as "Sponsored" may appear in your feed. These are targeted based on your activity, interests, and demographic information.

5. **Live Updates**

   o The News Feed updates in real-time, meaning new posts can appear while you're scrolling.

6. **Filters and Sorting**

   o You can adjust your feed preferences to sort by "Most Recent" or "Top Stories," ensuring the most relevant or newest content appears first.

How to Navigate the News Feed

1. **Accessing the News Feed**

   o When you log into Facebook, the News Feed is the default screen you see.

   o If you've navigated away, you can return to the News Feed by clicking the **home icon** (shaped like a house) on the top toolbar.

2. **Scrolling Through Posts**

   o Use your mouse, trackpad, or finger (if on a touchscreen device) to scroll down the feed.

   o Older posts will load as you continue scrolling.

3. **Interacting with Posts**

   o **Reacting to Posts:** Hover or tap the **like button** to access the full range of reactions.

   o **Commenting:** Click the "Comment" icon to leave your thoughts or respond to others.

   o **Sharing:** Use the "Share" button to repost content on your timeline, in a group, or via private message.

4. **Viewing Stories**

   o Stories appear as circles at the top of the News Feed. Click or tap a story to view it.

   o Stories autoplay, so once one ends, the next will begin. Swipe or click to move forward or backward.

5. **Exploring Posts in Detail**

   o Clicking on a post expands it, allowing you to see all comments, related media, and additional details.

Customizing Your News Feed Experience

1. **Adjusting Feed Preferences**

   o Click the **menu icon** (three horizontal lines) and go to **Settings & Privacy > News Feed Preferences** to customize what you see.

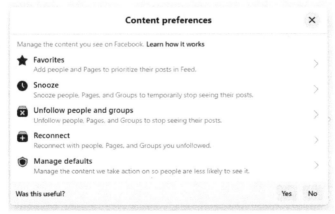

   o Options include:

   ▪ Prioritizing content from specific friends or pages.

- Unfollowing people or groups without unfriending.

- Reconnecting with unfollowed accounts.

2. **Sorting Your Feed**

   o By default, Facebook shows "Top Stories," but you can switch to "Most Recent."

   o On the top left of the News Feed, click the **three dots** beside "Feeds" and select your sorting preference.

3. **Hiding Unwanted Content**

   o If a post doesn't interest you, click the **three dots** at the top right of the post and choose "Hide Post" or "Snooze [user/page/group] for 30 days."

4. **Saving Posts**

   o To revisit a post later, click the **three dots** on the post and select "Save Post." Saved posts can be accessed via the **Saved** section in the menu.

5. **Exploring Feeds**

   o Use the filters in the left sidebar (on desktop) or the menu (on mobile) to view specific content categories, such as "Groups," "Pages," or "Friends."

Tips for Efficient Navigation

1. **Keyboard Shortcuts (Desktop)**

   o Use Facebook keyboard shortcuts for quicker navigation:

     ▪ Press **J** or **K** to scroll between posts.

     ▪ Press **L** to like a post.

     ▪ Press **Enter** to comment on a post.

2. **Search for Specific Content**

   o Use the search bar at the top to find posts, friends, groups, or pages.

3. **Stay Updated with Notifications**

   o Notifications keep you informed about new interactions. Click the **bell icon** to access your notifications and jump directly to the relevant content.

Best Practices for a Positive News Feed Experience

1. **Avoid Information Overload**

   o Follow only friends, groups, and pages that provide value.

   o Limit the time you spend scrolling to maintain a healthy social media balance.

2. **Engage Thoughtfully**

   o Comment and react to posts with meaningful input to foster better connections.

   o Avoid engaging in heated discussions or negative posts.

3. **Report and Block Harmful Content**

   o Use the reporting tools available in the **three-dot menu** to flag inappropriate or harmful posts.

   o Block or unfollow users or pages that consistently post undesirable content.

Conclusion

Mastering the News Feed allows you to maximize your Facebook experience, stay connected, and engage meaningfully with your network. By understanding its features, customizing your preferences, and using best practices, you can ensure that the content you see aligns with your interests and enhances your social media experience.

2.2.2 The Menu and Toolbar Explained

The Facebook menu and toolbar serve as the backbone of the platform's navigation system, providing access to its many features and tools. Understanding how to use the menu and toolbar effectively will significantly enhance your experience and allow you to navigate Facebook with ease. This section breaks down each component of the menu and toolbar, explaining its purpose and how to use it.

The Main Toolbar: Your Central Navigation Hub

The main toolbar is typically located at the top of the Facebook interface, whether you're using the mobile app or the desktop website. It provides quick access to the platform's most frequently used features. Let's explore each element in detail:

1. **Search Bar**

- o **Purpose:** The search bar allows you to quickly find people, pages, groups, events, or posts.

- o **How to Use:** Simply type in a keyword, such as a friend's name or a topic of interest. Facebook will display suggestions in real time, divided into categories like "People," "Pages," and "Groups." Select the desired result to navigate directly to it.

- o **Tips for Effective Search:**

  - ▪ Use specific keywords for more accurate results.

  - ▪ Use filters (e.g., "posts from friends" or "events near me") to narrow down your search.

2. **Home Icon**

- o **Purpose:** The home icon takes you back to your News Feed, where you can view posts and updates from friends, pages, and groups you follow.

- o **How to Use:** Click or tap the home icon at any time to return to the main feed. It's your go-to place for staying updated on what's happening in your network.

3. **Watch (Video Icon)**

- o **Purpose:** This section showcases video content, including live streams, trending videos, and videos from pages you follow.

- o **How to Use:**

    - Browse through suggested videos or search for specific ones.

    - You can like, comment, or share videos directly from this section.

    - Follow creators or pages for more personalized recommendations.

- o **Pro Tip:** Explore the "Watch Later" feature to save videos you want to view later.

4. **Marketplace (Shopping Bag Icon)**

- o **Purpose:** The Marketplace is a hub for buying and selling items locally.

- o **How to Use:**

  - Browse through categories like electronics, furniture, or clothing.

  - List your items for sale by uploading photos, writing descriptions, and setting prices.

- o **Pro Tip:** Use filters to search for items within specific price ranges or locations.

5. **Groups (Two People Icon)**

- o **Purpose:** Provides access to all groups you've joined, along with recommendations for new ones.

- o **How to Use:**

  - View updates from your groups by clicking the icon.

  - Join or create new groups that align with your interests.

  - Manage your group notifications to control the volume of updates you receive.

6. **Notifications (Bell Icon)**

o **Purpose:** Displays alerts about likes, comments, friend requests, and other interactions.

o **How to Use:**

- Click or tap the bell icon to view your recent notifications.

- Interact with notifications by clicking on them to open the related post, comment, or activity.

o **Pro Tip:** Customize your notification settings in the "Settings & Privacy" section to avoid being overwhelmed.

7. **Messenger (Chat Bubble Icon)**

o **Purpose:** Messenger is Facebook's built-in communication tool for chatting with friends.

o **How to Use:**

- Open the icon to view recent conversations.

- Start new chats by searching for a contact or selecting one from your list.

- Use features like stickers, voice messages, and video calls.

o **Pro Tip:** Download the standalone Messenger app for additional features, such as secret conversations and offline messaging.

8. **Profile Icon**

o **Purpose:** Clicking on your profile icon takes you directly to your Facebook profile page.

o **How to Use:**

- View and edit your profile information, including your bio, photos, and timeline posts.

- Use the "Activity Log" to review your interactions on Facebook.

o **Pro Tip:** Regularly update your profile to keep it current and engaging for friends and visitors.

The Sidebar Menu: Access to All Features

On the desktop version, the left-hand sidebar serves as an extended menu, while on mobile devices, this menu is accessible via the three horizontal lines ("hamburger icon"). This section includes additional features and settings.

1. **Your Shortcuts**

- o **Purpose:** Displays a customizable list of your most-used features, such as groups, pages, or events.

- o **How to Use:**

    - Pin frequently accessed features for quick navigation.

    - Rearrange shortcuts by dragging and dropping them in the order you prefer.

2. **Explore**

    - o **Purpose:** Provides access to features like Facebook Watch, Marketplace, and Gaming.

    - o **How to Use:**

- Browse each category to discover new content, events, or communities.
- Use the Gaming section to find and play games directly within Facebook.

3. **Saved**

   o **Purpose:** Displays posts, videos, or links you've saved for later viewing.

   o **How to Use:**

   - Save content by clicking the three dots on a post and selecting "Save."
   - Access saved items in this section whenever you're ready to revisit them.

4. **Events**

   o **Purpose:** View upcoming events or create new ones.

   o **How to Use:**

   - RSVP to events you're interested in.
   - Use filters to discover events happening nearby or hosted by friends.

5. **Pages**

   o **Purpose:** Displays pages you've liked or created.

   o **How to Use:**

   - Manage your pages by posting updates, interacting with followers, or viewing insights.

Advanced Features in the Toolbar

1. **Settings & Privacy**

   o **Purpose:** Allows you to customize your account settings and control privacy preferences.

   o **How to Use:**

      ▪ Access "Settings & Privacy" from the toolbar dropdown menu.

      ▪ Adjust settings for privacy, notifications, and account security.

   o **Pro Tip:** Use the "Privacy Checkup" tool to review and adjust key privacy settings in minutes.

2. **Help & Support**

   o **Purpose:** Offers resources for troubleshooting and learning more about Facebook features.

   o **How to Use:**

      ▪ Visit the Help Center to search for answers to common questions.

      ▪ Report issues or send feedback directly to Facebook.

3. **Dark Mode**

- o **Purpose:** Switches the interface to a darker color scheme, which can be easier on the eyes.

- o **How to Use:**

    - Toggle "Dark Mode" on or off in the "Settings & Privacy" section.

Tips for Mastering the Menu and Toolbar

- **Practice Navigation:** Spend time exploring each section to become familiar with its layout and features.

- **Customize Your Experience:** Adjust shortcuts, notifications, and privacy settings to suit your preferences.

- **Use Keyboard Shortcuts:** On desktop, shortcuts like "Alt + 1" for the News Feed or "Alt + 2" for your profile can save time.

By mastering the Facebook menu and toolbar, you'll be able to navigate the platform confidently and take full advantage of its features. Whether you're exploring groups, managing your notifications, or engaging with your network, the menu and toolbar are the keys to a seamless Facebook experience.

2.2.3 Managing Notifications

Notifications are one of the most crucial features of Facebook, helping you stay updated on activities, interactions, and important events. They serve as alerts for activities like comments on your posts, reactions, friend requests, group updates, and much more. Managing your notifications effectively ensures you're not overwhelmed while staying informed about what matters most to you. This section will guide you through everything you need to know about notifications: how they work, how to customize them, and how to minimize distractions.

---

1. Types of Facebook Notifications

Facebook offers different types of notifications depending on the platform you are using. Understanding these will help you decide which notifications you want to keep active:

1. **Push Notifications**: These are alerts sent directly to your device, appearing on your phone's lock screen or desktop. They notify you in real-time about new activity, like a friend request or someone tagging you in a post.

2. **In-App Notifications**: These appear within the Facebook app or website, usually as a red badge icon on the notification bell in the top menu bar.

3. **Email Notifications**: Facebook can send you email updates about account activity. For example, if someone tags you in a photo, you may receive an email alert.

4. **SMS Notifications**: If you've linked your phone number to your account, Facebook can send notifications via text message. This feature is less common but still useful for specific scenarios.

---

2. How to Access Your Notifications

Managing your notifications starts with understanding where to find them. Follow these steps:

1. **On Desktop**
   - Log in to your Facebook account.
   - Look for the bell icon in the top right corner of the screen.
   - Click on it to open the Notifications tab, where you can see a chronological list of updates.

2. **On Mobile**
   - Open the Facebook app on your smartphone.
   - Tap the bell icon at the top of the screen (for iOS) or in the menu bar (for Android).
   - This will open a list of your most recent notifications.

3. **Notification Preferences**
   - Click or tap on a notification to view the related content, such as a comment or post.

   o   You can also swipe left on mobile to archive or manage individual notifications.

---

3. Customizing Notification Settings

Customizing notifications is essential for tailoring your Facebook experience. Here's how to do it step-by-step:

Adjusting Notification Settings on Desktop

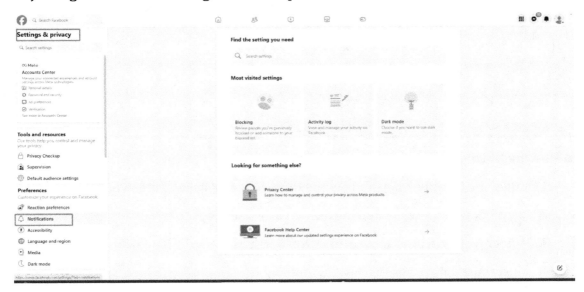

1. Click on your profile picture in the top right corner.

2. Select **Settings & Privacy > Settings**.

3. In the left-hand menu, click **Notifications**.

4. From here, you can manage notifications for specific categories like:

   o   **Comments**: Get notified when someone comments on your posts.

   o   **Tags**: Receive alerts when someone tags you in a post or photo.

   o   **Friend Requests**: Control whether you're notified of new friend requests.

   o   **Birthdays**: Get reminders about your friends' birthdays.

5. Toggle the notification switch for each category to turn notifications on or off.

Adjusting Notification Settings on Mobile

1. Open the Facebook app and tap the three horizontal lines (menu button).

2. Scroll down and select **Settings & Privacy** > **Settings**.

3. Under **Notifications**, tap **Notification Settings**.

4. Customize categories such as:

   o **Push Notifications**: Control alerts sent to your phone.

   o **Email Notifications**: Choose whether you want email updates.

   o **SMS Notifications**: Enable or disable text message alerts.

5. For each category, tap to expand and modify individual settings.

4. Turning Off Notifications for Specific Activities

If you find certain notifications unnecessary or distracting, you can turn them off for specific activities:

Muting Notifications for a Post

- Go to the post you want to mute.

- Click the three dots in the top-right corner of the post.

- Select **Turn off notifications for this post**.

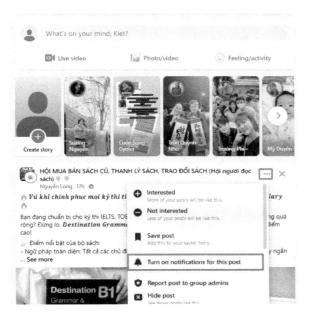

Stopping Notifications for Groups or Pages

1. Visit the group or page.

2. Tap the **Joined** button (for groups) or the **Following** button (for pages).

3. Select **Manage Notifications** and adjust your preferences.

HỘI CƯ DÂN D-AQUA QUẬN 8 - KÊNH THÔNG TIN BẤT ĐỘNG SẢN

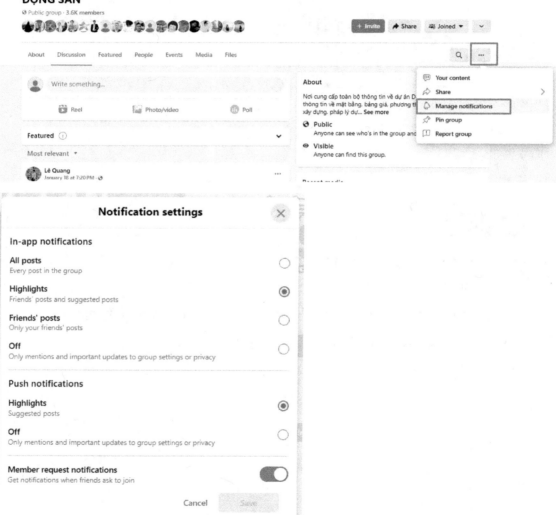

Limiting Event Notifications

1. Open the Events tab.

2. Find the event you want to manage.

3. Tap the three dots next to the event and select **Turn off notifications**.

5. Managing Notification Frequency

Facebook allows you to control how often you receive notifications:

Setting Notification Frequency

1. Navigate to **Settings & Privacy** > **Settings** > **Notifications**.

2. Under each category, you'll see an option to choose how frequently you want notifications (e.g., immediately, daily, or weekly summaries).

3. Adjust based on your preferences to reduce unnecessary alerts.

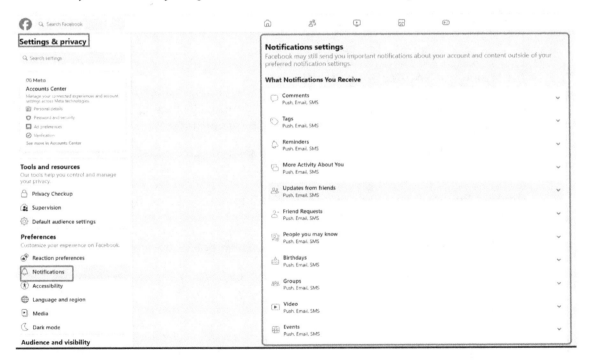

6. Troubleshooting Notification Issues

Sometimes, notifications might not work as expected. Here are common problems and solutions:

Notifications Not Showing Up

- Ensure notifications are enabled in your device's settings.
- Check your internet connection.

Receiving Too Many Notifications

- Review and adjust your notification settings to eliminate unnecessary alerts.
- Unfollow groups or pages that send excessive updates.

Notifications Appearing Late

- Update your Facebook app to the latest version.
- Clear your browser cache if you're using Facebook on desktop.

7. Tips for Managing Notifications Effectively

- **Prioritize Important Updates**: Customize settings to highlight notifications that matter most, such as messages, comments, or group activity.
- **Limit Push Notifications**: Disable non-essential push alerts to avoid constant distractions.
- **Review Regularly**: Periodically review and update your notification preferences to reflect changing priorities.
- **Use Quiet Mode**: Schedule quiet hours to focus on tasks without interruptions.
- **Engage Selectively**: Avoid clicking on every notification. Instead, focus on the most relevant ones to save time.

By understanding and managing notifications effectively, you can streamline your Facebook experience. Whether you're looking to stay updated on friends and family or focusing on specific groups and pages, these tips will help you stay informed without feeling overwhelmed.

2.3 Securing Your Account

2.3.1 Setting Up Two-Factor Authentication

Two-Factor Authentication (2FA) is one of the most effective ways to secure your Facebook account. By enabling 2FA, you add an additional layer of security, making it much harder for unauthorized users to gain access to your account, even if they know your password. This section provides a comprehensive, step-by-step guide to understanding, enabling, and managing Two-Factor Authentication on Facebook.

What is Two-Factor Authentication?

Two-Factor Authentication is a security measure that requires you to verify your identity using two different factors:

1. **Something you know** – Your Facebook password.

2. **Something you have** – A secondary verification method, such as a one-time code sent to your phone or generated by an app.

This ensures that even if someone manages to steal your password, they cannot access your account without the second factor of authentication.

Why Enable Two-Factor Authentication?

Enabling 2FA provides several benefits:

- **Enhanced Security**: Prevent unauthorized access to your account, even if your password is compromised.

- **Peace of Mind**: Receive real-time alerts if someone tries to log in from an unrecognized device or location.

- **Compliance with Best Practices**: Many websites and services recommend or require 2FA for better protection.

How to Enable Two-Factor Authentication on Facebook

Follow these steps to set up Two-Factor Authentication on your Facebook account:

Step 1: Access the Security Settings

1. Log in to your Facebook account.

2. Click on the **profile picture** in the top-right corner of the screen.

3. Select **Settings & Privacy**, then click on **Settings**.

4. On the left-hand menu, click **Password and security**.

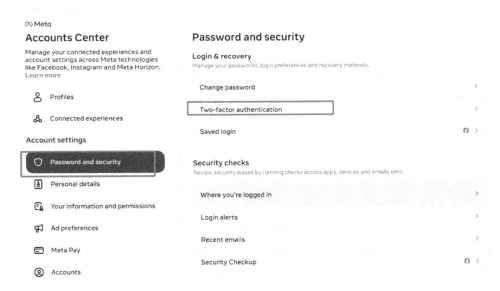

Step 2: Locate Two-Factor Authentication

1. Under the "Security and Login" section, find the **Two-Factor Authentication** option.

2. Click on **Edit** or **Set Up** next to this option.

Step 3: Choose Your Security Method

Facebook provides several methods for Two-Factor Authentication. Choose the one that works best for you:

- **Authentication App**: Use apps like Google Authenticator, Authy, or Duo Mobile to generate a one-time code.

- **Text Message (SMS)**: Receive a one-time code sent to your phone via SMS.

- **Security Key**: Use a physical USB or NFC security key (for advanced users).

Step 4: Set Up Your Preferred Method

1. **Using an Authentication App**:

   o Select **Authentication App** as your preferred method.

   o Facebook will display a QR code.

   o Open your authentication app and scan the QR code, or manually enter the setup key provided.

   o The app will generate a six-digit code. Enter this code on Facebook to complete the setup.

2. **Using SMS Verification**:

   o Select **Text Message** as your method.

   o Enter your phone number and click **Continue**.

   o Facebook will send a one-time code to your phone. Enter the code to verify your number.

3. **Using a Security Key**:

   o Select **Security Key** and follow the on-screen instructions to connect and register your USB or NFC key.

   o Insert your security key into your device when prompted to verify and activate it.

Step 5: Confirm and Activate 2FA

Once you've set up your chosen method, Facebook will ask you to confirm the setup by sending a test code.

1. Enter the test code you receive or generate.

2. Click **Finish** to activate Two-Factor Authentication.

Additional Features for Two-Factor Authentication

After enabling 2FA, Facebook provides additional options to enhance your account security:

Backup Codes

- Facebook generates a set of one-time backup codes. These codes can be used if you lose access to your primary authentication method.

- Save these codes in a secure location, such as a password manager or a physical notebook.

Trusted Contacts

- Add a few trusted friends who can help you regain access to your account in case you're locked out.

- To set this up, go to **Security and Login > Choose 3 to 5 Friends to Contact if You Get Locked Out**.

Login Alerts

- Turn on notifications for unrecognized logins. This way, you'll be alerted if someone tries to access your account from a new device or location.

Best Practices for Managing Two-Factor Authentication

Keep Your Devices Secure

- Ensure your smartphone, where you receive codes or use authentication apps, is protected by a strong PIN or biometric security.

- Avoid sharing your phone or authentication app with others.

Regularly Update Recovery Options

- Update your phone number if it changes.

- Revisit and refresh your backup codes periodically.

Beware of Phishing Attempts

- Facebook will never ask you for your login codes via email or text.

- Always verify the source of messages before entering any codes.

Use a Password Manager

- Store your backup codes and other credentials securely in a reliable password manager.

Troubleshooting Common Issues with Two-Factor Authentication

What if I Lose Access to My 2FA Method?

1. Use one of your backup codes to log in.

2. Contact your trusted contacts to help you regain access.

3. Use Facebook's account recovery options by visiting the **Help Center**.

What if My SMS Code Doesn't Arrive?

1. Check that your phone number is correct.

2. Ensure your phone has good network coverage.

3. Try using an authentication app instead of SMS.

Can I Disable Two-Factor Authentication?

Yes, but it's not recommended. To disable 2FA, return to the "Security and Login" settings and follow the prompts to turn it off.

Conclusion

Setting up Two-Factor Authentication on Facebook is a critical step in protecting your account from unauthorized access. By taking a few minutes to enable and configure this feature, you significantly reduce the risk of your account being compromised. Stay vigilant, keep your recovery options updated, and enjoy a more secure Facebook experience.

2.3.2 Privacy Settings Overview

When using Facebook, one of the most critical aspects of maintaining your online safety and personal comfort is understanding and utilizing its privacy settings effectively. Facebook provides a wide array of options to help users control who sees their information, how they interact with others, and what they share on the platform. This section will walk you through an in-depth overview of Facebook's privacy settings, how to navigate them, and best practices for customizing these settings to suit your needs.

Why Privacy Settings Matter

Privacy settings on Facebook allow you to manage the visibility of your personal information, posts, and activities. By adjusting these settings, you can:

- Protect sensitive personal information from strangers.

- Avoid unwanted friend requests, messages, or interactions.

- Prevent unauthorized access to your photos, videos, and posts.

- Maintain control over how your profile appears to others.

Ignoring these settings could lead to exposure of your personal details to people you do not trust, making you vulnerable to privacy breaches, scams, or even identity theft.

Navigating to Privacy Settings

To begin customizing your privacy settings, follow these steps:

1. **Access the Settings Menu:**

   o Open Facebook on your browser or app.

   o Click on your profile picture or the downward arrow in the top-right corner.

   o Select **"Settings & Privacy"** and then click on **"Privacy Checkup"** or **"Settings."**

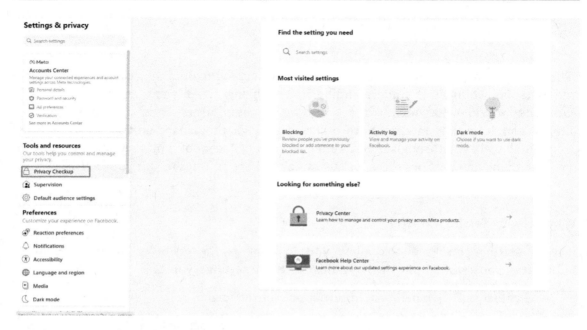

2. **Locate the Privacy Tab:**

    o   In the settings menu, find and click on the **"Privacy"** tab on the left-hand side (on desktop) or under "Settings" (on mobile).

    o   This section contains all the privacy-related options categorized for ease of use.

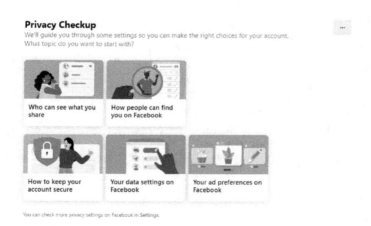

Key Privacy Settings to Review

1. **Who Can See Your Posts and Profile Information**

    o **Setting Visibility for Future Posts:**

        ▪ Go to the **"Your Activity"** section.

        ▪ Under **"Who can see your future posts?"**, choose your preferred audience: Public, Friends, Friends Except..., Specific Friends, or Only Me.

        ▪ If you want to hide your posts from specific people, select **"Friends Except..."** and add their names.

    o **Adjusting Past Post Visibility:**

        ▪ Use the **"Limit Past Posts"** option to change the visibility of older posts from Public or Friends of Friends to just Friends.

    o **Managing Profile Information Visibility:**

        ▪ Edit your profile by clicking the **"About"** section.

        ▪ Adjust the visibility of each detail (e.g., phone number, email address, relationship status) using the privacy dropdown next to each field.

2. **Who Can Send You Friend Requests**

    o In the **"How People Find and Contact You"** section, you can limit who can send you friend requests:

        ▪ Options include **Everyone** or **Friends of Friends.**

        ▪ Selecting **Friends of Friends** significantly reduces the chances of receiving spam or unwanted requests.

3. **Who Can Look You Up**

    o Decide if others can find your profile using your email address or phone number:

        ▪ In **"How People Find and Contact You,"** look for the options:

- - Who can look you up using the email address you provided?

    - Who can look you up using the phone number you provided?

  - Set these to **Friends** or **Only Me** for maximum privacy.

4. **Search Engine Linking**

   o By default, Facebook allows search engines like Google to link to your profile.

   o To disable this:

     - In **"Privacy Settings,"** scroll to **"Do you want search engines outside of Facebook to link to your profile?"**

     - Turn this option **off** to prevent your profile from appearing in search engine results.

Controlling Tags and Mentions

Facebook allows users to tag others in posts, photos, and comments. While this can be a fun feature, it may expose your profile or photos to unintended audiences. To manage this:

1. **Review Tags Before They Appear on Your Profile**

   o Go to the **"Profile and Tagging"** section in the privacy settings.

   o Enable the option to **"Review posts you're tagged in before the post appears on your profile."**

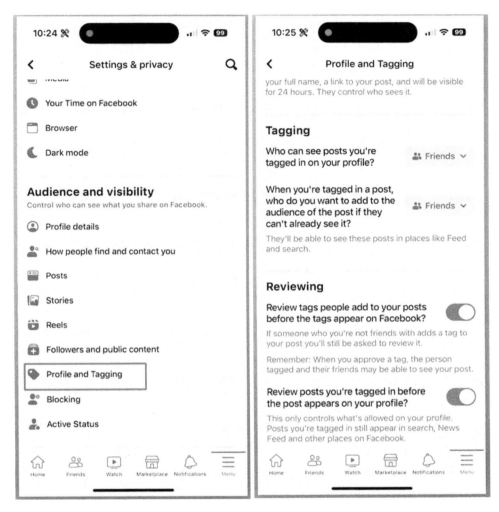

2. **Control Who Can Tag You**

   o Adjust the setting under **"Who can see posts you're tagged in on your profile?"**

   o Choose an audience such as Friends or Only Me.

3. **Review Photos You're Tagged In**

   o Use the **Activity Log** to review all posts and photos you've been tagged in.

   o Un-tag yourself from posts you don't want associated with your profile.

Blocking and Reporting

1. **Using the Block Feature**

    o   Facebook allows you to block users who may be harassing or annoying you.

    o   When you block someone:

        ▪   They cannot see your profile or contact you.

        ▪   You won't see their content in your feed either.

    o   To block someone:

        ▪   Go to their profile, click on the three dots ("**...**") in the top-right corner, and select **"Block."**

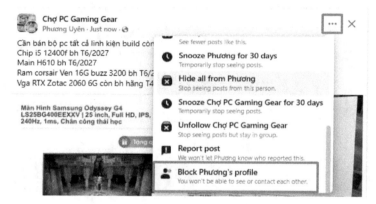

2. **Reporting Problematic Content**

    o   If you encounter inappropriate or abusive posts, profiles, or messages, report them:

        ▪   Click on the three dots next to the content.

        ▪   Choose **"Find Support or Report Post."**

        ▪   Follow the prompts to submit a report to Facebook's team.

Best Practices for Maintaining Privacy

1. **Regularly Review Your Privacy Settings**

   o   Facebook often updates its privacy policies and features, so it's a good habit to review your settings every few months.

2. **Be Cautious About Public Posts**

   o   Before posting, think about whether the content is appropriate for a wide audience.

3. **Use Strong Passwords**

   o   Combine letters, numbers, and special characters for a strong password. Avoid using the same password across multiple platforms.

4. **Enable Login Alerts**

   o   In the **"Security and Login"** section, enable alerts for unrecognized logins.

5. **Educate Yourself About New Features**

   o   Stay informed about Facebook's new tools or privacy options to ensure you're fully protected.

Conclusion

Facebook's privacy settings are designed to give you control over your digital presence. By taking the time to customize these settings, you can create a safer, more comfortable environment for yourself on the platform. Regularly reviewing and updating your preferences ensures you stay one step ahead of potential privacy risks.

2.3.3 Recognizing and Avoiding Scams

As one of the most popular social media platforms in the world, Facebook unfortunately attracts scammers and cybercriminals looking to exploit users for personal information, financial gain, or malicious purposes. Recognizing and avoiding scams is critical to ensuring your safety and security while using Facebook. In this section, we'll explore common types of Facebook scams, how to spot them, and actionable steps to protect yourself.

Understanding Common Facebook Scams

1. **Phishing Scams**: Phishing scams are among the most common types of cyberattacks on Facebook. These involve fake messages or links designed to trick you into providing sensitive information, such as your login credentials or credit card details. Scammers may send messages that appear to come from Facebook itself, asking you to "verify your account" or "reset your password."

How to Spot Phishing Scams:

- o Look for grammatical errors or unusual phrasing in the message.

- o Check the sender's email address or username. Genuine Facebook communications will come from a "@facebook.com" domain.

- o Avoid clicking on suspicious links, especially if they direct you to a website that doesn't start with "https://" or lacks the Facebook logo.

- o Be cautious if the message creates a sense of urgency, such as "Your account will be suspended unless you act immediately."

2. **Fake Friend Requests**: Scammers often create fake profiles to send friend requests to unsuspecting users. Once accepted, they may try to gain your trust, ask for money, or share malicious links.

Signs of a Fake Profile:

- o The profile has only a few photos or posts.

- o The account was recently created.

- o The profile picture looks like a stock image or is suspiciously professional.

- o They have no mutual friends or an unusually high number of random connections.

3. **Prize or Lottery Scams**: These scams promise large cash rewards, gift cards, or other prizes in exchange for a "small processing fee" or personal information. Scammers may claim you've won a contest that you never entered or that Facebook is giving away money to loyal users.

How to Identify a Fake Prize Offer:

- o The message comes from an unofficial account or page.

- o You are asked to provide sensitive information such as your address or credit card details.
- o The prize seems too good to be true.

4. **Job Offer Scams**: Fraudulent job offers often circulate on Facebook, promising high salaries for minimal work. These scams typically request upfront payments for "training materials" or "registration fees."

How to Verify Job Offers:

- o Research the company to ensure it's legitimate.
- o Avoid offers that require payment or personal financial details upfront.
- o Be skeptical of job posts that lack professional formatting or include vague descriptions.

5. **Charity Scams**: Scammers exploit users' goodwill by creating fake charity campaigns, often related to natural disasters or humanitarian crises.

Tips to Identify Fake Charities:

- o Verify the organization's legitimacy through trusted websites like Charity Navigator or GuideStar.
- o Be wary of emotional appeals combined with demands for immediate donations.
- o Avoid donating directly through Facebook links unless they are part of verified fundraisers.

How to Protect Yourself from Facebook Scams

1. **Enable Strong Privacy Settings**

- o Limit who can see your posts, photos, and friend list by customizing your privacy settings.
- o Restrict the ability of strangers to send you friend requests by selecting "Friends of Friends" under "Who can send you friend requests?" in your settings.

2. **Be Skeptical of Unsolicited Messages**

   o Avoid engaging with messages from unknown users, especially if they contain links or requests for information.

   o Report suspicious messages by clicking on the three-dot menu and selecting "Report Message."

3. **Verify Links Before Clicking**

   o Hover over links to preview the URL before clicking. Ensure that the link starts with "https://" and is associated with Facebook or a trusted site.

   o If you're unsure about a link, don't click on it. Instead, navigate directly to the website through your browser.

4. **Educate Yourself About Scams**

   o Stay informed about the latest types of scams circulating on Facebook. Facebook's Help Center frequently updates information on identifying and avoiding scams.

   o Participate in online forums or cybersecurity workshops to learn more about safe internet practices.

5. **Use Two-Factor Authentication (2FA)**

   o Enable 2FA to add an extra layer of protection to your account. This ensures that even if someone has your password, they can't access your account without the second authentication factor.

   o Use a reliable authentication app such as Google Authenticator or Authy for added security.

6. **Report Suspicious Activity**

   o If you encounter a fake profile, phishing attempt, or scam message, report it to Facebook immediately.

   o To report a profile, go to their page, click on the three-dot menu, and select "Find support or report profile."

7. **Avoid Sharing Sensitive Information Online**

o Never share your Social Security number, financial details, or passwords through Facebook messages or posts.

o Be cautious when sharing personal details, such as your full name, address, or phone number, even in private groups.

What to Do If You've Been Targeted by a Scam

1. **Change Your Password Immediately**: If you suspect your account has been compromised, update your password immediately. Choose a strong password with a mix of letters, numbers, and symbols.

2. **Enable Account Recovery Options**

   o Make sure your recovery email and phone number are up-to-date. This will help you regain access if your account is hacked.

3. **Check Your Login Activity**

   o Go to "Settings & Privacy" > "Activity log" to view where your account is currently logged in. Log out of any unfamiliar devices.

4. **Contact Facebook Support**

- o If you believe your account has been hacked, visit Facebook's Help Center for guidance on account recovery.

5. **Notify Your Friends**

- o Warn your Facebook friends if you think a scammer has impersonated you or used your account to send fraudulent messages.

Conclusion

Facebook is an incredible tool for connecting with others, but it's essential to remain vigilant about potential scams. By learning how to recognize suspicious activities and implementing best practices for online security, you can protect yourself and enjoy a safer experience on the platform. Remember, when in doubt, always prioritize caution over convenience. Facebook offers numerous tools to help you stay safe—make use of them and empower yourself to navigate the digital world with confidence.

CHAPTER II
Building Your Network

3.1 Finding and Adding Friends

3.1.1 Sending and Accepting Friend Requests

In this section, we will explore the detailed process of sending and accepting friend requests on Facebook. Whether you're new to Facebook or looking to expand your social network, understanding this feature is essential for building meaningful connections. Let's break it down into easy-to-follow steps.

Understanding Friend Requests

Before diving into the step-by-step instructions, it's important to understand what friend requests are and how they function. Friend requests allow you to connect with people on Facebook by adding them to your friends list. Once someone accepts your request, you can see their posts, interact with their content, and communicate via private messages. Similarly, they gain access to your content, depending on your privacy settings.

When you send a friend request, the recipient has three options:

- **Accept**: The person accepts your request, and you both become friends on Facebook.

- **Decline**: The person chooses not to connect, and your request is rejected.

- **Ignore**: The person decides not to respond but does not explicitly decline the request.

Facebook also has built-in features to help you manage friend requests effectively. Let's move on to the practical steps.

Step-by-Step Guide to Sending Friend Requests

Step 1: Find the Person You Want to Add

1. **Search Using the Facebook Search Bar**

   o At the top of your Facebook homepage or app, locate the search bar.

   o Type the name of the person you want to connect with. If the name is common, add additional details like their location, workplace, or school to narrow your search.

   o Press the search icon or hit enter.

2. **Browse Through the Search Results**

    o   Facebook will display a list of profiles that match your search. Look for the person's profile picture, mutual friends, or other identifying details to ensure it's the correct person.

    o   If the person's profile is private, you may only see limited information.

3. **Click on the Profile**

    o   Once you find the right profile, click on their name or profile picture to visit their profile page.

Step 2: Send the Friend Request

1. **Locate the "Add Friend" Button**

    o   On the person's profile, you'll see an **"Add Friend"** button near their name or cover photo.

    o   Click or tap the button to send the friend request.

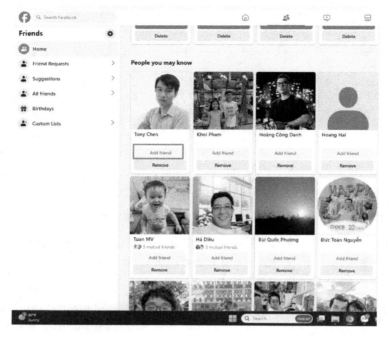

2. **Wait for Confirmation**

   o   After sending the request, the button will change to **"Friend Request Sent."** This means the request is pending and awaiting the recipient's response.

   o   You cannot send another request to the same person unless they decline your first request.

Step 3: Track Sent Requests (Optional)

If you want to review the requests you've sent:

- **On the Desktop Version**:

  o   Click on the **Friends** icon in the top right corner of your Facebook homepage.

  o   Select **View Sent Requests** to see all pending friend requests.

- **On the Mobile App**:

  o   Tap the **Friends** icon at the bottom of the screen.

  o   Navigate to the **Outgoing Requests** section.

Etiquette Tips for Sending Friend Requests

- **Be Selective**: Only send requests to people you know or have a legitimate reason to connect with.

- **Avoid Spamming**: Sending requests to too many strangers in a short period may result in your account being flagged by Facebook.

- **Include a Message**: If the person might not recognize you immediately, consider sending a polite message introducing yourself along with the request.

Step-by-Step Guide to Accepting Friend Requests

Step 1: Access Your Friend Requests

1. **On the Desktop Version**:
   - Click on the **Friends** icon in the top right corner of the screen.
   - A dropdown menu will appear showing pending friend requests.

2. **On the Mobile App**:
   - Tap the **Friends** icon at the bottom of the app interface.
   - Navigate to the **Requests** section to see incoming friend requests.

Step 2: Review the Request

1. **Check the Profile**
   - Click or tap on the person's name to visit their profile before accepting.
   - Look for mutual friends, shared interests, or other details to confirm you know them or want to connect.

2. **Verify Legitimacy**
   - Be cautious of fake profiles. Look for warning signs like generic profile pictures, vague information, or overly friendly messages.

Step 3: Accept or Decline the Request

1. **Accepting a Request**

- o If you decide to accept, click or tap the **"Confirm"** button next to the request.

- o Once accepted, the person will be added to your friends list, and you'll see their posts on your News Feed.

2. **Declining a Request**

- o If you do not want to connect, click or tap the **"Delete Request"** option.

- o Facebook will not notify the person that you declined their request.

Optional: Blocking or Reporting Suspicious Requests

If you receive a friend request from someone suspicious, you can block or report the profile:

- Go to their profile and click the **three dots menu**.

- Select **"Block"** or **"Report"** and follow the on-screen instructions.

Common Issues and How to Resolve Them

1. **Can't Find the "Add Friend" Button**

- o This might occur if the person has restricted who can send them friend requests (e.g., only mutual friends).

2. **Friend Request Limit Reached**

- o Facebook limits users to 5,000 friends. If either you or the recipient has reached this limit, you won't be able to send or accept new requests.

3. **Request Declined Without Notification**

- o Facebook does not notify you if someone declines your request, so avoid sending repeated requests to the same person.

Best Practices for Sending and Accepting Friend Requests

1. **Personalize Your Requests**

  o If appropriate, send a message explaining why you're reaching out. For example:
   "Hi [Name], I came across your profile and noticed we have mutual interests in [topic]. I'd love to connect!"

2. **Respect Boundaries**

  o Not everyone may want to accept your request. Be respectful and avoid pressuring others to connect.

3. **Maintain Privacy**

  o Regularly review your privacy settings to control who can send you friend requests.

By following these steps and tips, you'll be able to navigate the friend request process confidently, expanding your network while ensuring meaningful and secure connections.

3.1.2 Managing Your Friends List

Managing your friends list on Facebook is an essential skill for maintaining a personalized, relevant, and secure social media experience. By organizing, reviewing, and optimizing your connections, you can ensure a healthier balance between online socialization and privacy. This section provides a comprehensive guide to understanding and managing your Facebook friends list effectively.

Understanding Your Friends List

Your friends list is the foundation of your Facebook network. It consists of everyone you've connected with on the platform. Here's why managing it is important:

- **Stay Organized:** Keep your interactions meaningful by decluttering your list and focusing on people who matter most.

- **Protect Your Privacy:** Ensure that only trusted people have access to your shared posts and personal information.

- **Enhance Your Experience:** See relevant updates and avoid content from people you no longer interact with.

Accessing Your Friends List

To start managing your friends, you need to know how to access the list. Follow these steps:

1. Log in to your Facebook account.

2. Click on your **profile picture** in the top-right corner to go to your profile.

3. On your profile page, click the **Friends** tab. This opens a list of all your current connections.

4. From here, you can view, search, and manage your friends.

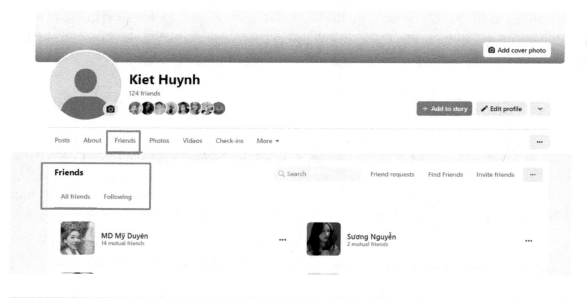

Categorizing Your Friends

Facebook allows you to categorize your friends into lists, making it easier to manage how you interact with them and what content they see.

Default Friend Lists: Facebook provides a few pre-set lists to help organize your network:

- **Close Friends:** People you want to see updates from frequently.

- **Acquaintances:** People whose posts you'd like to see less often.

- **Restricted:** Friends who can only see your public posts.

Creating Custom Friend Lists: If the default lists don't suit your needs, you can create custom lists.

1. Go to the **Friends** tab on your profile.

2. Click on **Custom Lists** or **Edit Lists**.

3. Select **Create List**, give it a name, and add friends to it.

4. Use these lists to filter your News Feed or control the audience for specific posts.

Adding or Removing Friends from Lists

To assign a friend to a specific list:

1. Go to your **Friends** tab.

2. Find the friend you want to manage.

3. Click the **three dots** next to their name and select **Edit Friend List**.

4. Choose a category (Close Friends, Acquaintances, or a custom list).

To remove a friend from a list, simply uncheck the list name.

Unfriending vs. Unfollowing

Sometimes, you may want to reduce your interactions with certain people. Facebook offers two options:

1. **Unfriending:**

    o When you unfriend someone, they are removed from your friends list, and you are removed from theirs.

    o They will not receive a notification, but they might notice if they visit your profile.

    o Use this option for people you no longer wish to connect with.

How to Unfriend:

- o Go to the **Friends** tab on your profile.

- o Find the person you want to unfriend.

- o Click the **Friends** button next to their name, then select **Unfriend**.

2. **Unfollowing:**

- o If you don't want to see someone's posts but wish to remain friends, unfollowing is a better option.

- o This action doesn't remove them from your friends list, and they won't be notified.

How to Unfollow:

- o Visit the profile of the person you wish to unfollow.

- o Click the **Following** button and select **Unfollow**.

Checking for Inactive or Duplicate Accounts

Over time, your friends list may accumulate inactive or duplicate accounts. Cleaning these up improves your experience.

How to Identify Inactive Accounts:

1. Go to your **Friends** list.

2. Look for profiles without profile pictures or those that haven't been active for a long time.

3. Decide whether to keep or unfriend these accounts.

Dealing with Duplicate Accounts: If a friend has multiple accounts, confirm with them which one is active before deciding to unfriend or unfollow the others.

Using Privacy Settings to Manage Friends

Your friends list visibility and the content they can see are controlled through Facebook's privacy settings.

1. **Hiding Your Friends List:**

    o   Navigate to **Settings & Privacy > Privacy Settings**.

    o   Under the **How People Find and Contact You** section, click **Who can see your friends list?**

    o   Choose from options like **Only Me**, **Friends**, or a custom audience.

2. **Customizing Post Visibility:**

   o When posting, use the audience selector to choose who can see your content.

   o Options include **Public**, **Friends**, or specific friend lists.

Using Friend Suggestions Wisely

Facebook frequently suggests friends based on mutual connections and interests. While these suggestions can be helpful, it's essential to review them critically to avoid adding people you don't know or trust.

Best Practices for Managing Your Friends List

To maintain a well-organized and meaningful friends list, consider these tips:

1. **Review Your List Regularly:** Periodically check your friends list to remove inactive or unwanted connections.

2. **Avoid Adding Strangers:** Only connect with people you know or have a legitimate reason to interact with.

3. **Engage with Your Close Friends:** Strengthen connections by liking, commenting, and messaging them.

4. **Monitor Friend Requests:** Accept requests only from people you recognize.

Conclusion

Managing your friends list on Facebook is not just about decluttering; it's about creating a secure and enjoyable social media environment. By categorizing your connections, customizing privacy settings, and staying mindful of your online interactions, you can make the most of your Facebook experience.

3.2 Joining Groups and Communities

3.2.1 Searching for Relevant Groups

Facebook Groups offer a fantastic way to connect with like-minded individuals, learn new things, and build meaningful relationships within various communities. Whether you're looking to join a group related to your hobbies, professional interests, or a shared cause, finding the right groups is the first step toward engaging effectively on Facebook. This section will guide you step-by-step on how to search for relevant groups and maximize your experience.

Understanding Facebook Groups

Before diving into the process of searching for groups, it's important to understand what Facebook Groups are and how they differ from other features, such as Pages. Groups are virtual communities where people with shared interests can come together to discuss topics, share updates, and collaborate. Unlike Pages, which are often created by businesses or public figures, Groups are usually more interactive and community-focused.

Facebook Groups come in three types of privacy settings:

- **Public Groups**: Anyone can find the group and view the posts within it.

- **Private Groups**: Only members can view posts. However, the group name and description may still be visible to non-members.

- **Hidden Groups**: These are invisible to non-members and can only be joined by invitation.

How to Search for Relevant Groups

1. Define Your Purpose

Before you start searching, take a moment to consider why you want to join a Facebook Group. Are you looking to:

- Connect with people who share a specific hobby or interest?

- Learn new skills or gain professional knowledge?

- Support a cause or engage in a community initiative?

- Network with people in your industry?

Clearly defining your purpose will help you filter through the millions of groups on Facebook and identify the ones that align with your needs.

2. Using the Facebook Search Bar

The Facebook search bar is one of the most efficient tools for finding groups. Here's how you can use it:

1. **Go to the Search Bar:** On the top of the Facebook interface (on both desktop and mobile), you'll see the search bar.

2. **Enter Keywords:** Type in specific keywords related to the type of group you want to join. For example:

   o If you're looking for cooking groups, type "Cooking" or "Recipes."

   o For professional networking, try "Marketing Professionals" or "Graphic Designers."

   o Add specific interests or locations, such as "Hiking in California" or "Freelancers in Asia."

3. **Select the 'Groups' Tab:** After typing your keyword, press Enter. You'll see a series of results that include Pages, posts, and groups. Click on the "Groups" tab to narrow the results to only groups.

4. **Review Group Listings:** Each result will show the group name, privacy type (Public or Private), and a brief description. You'll also see details such as the number of members and the most recent activity, which can indicate how active the group is.

3. Filtering Your Results

Facebook offers filtering options to refine your group search. After entering your keyword and selecting the "Groups" tab, you can use the following filters:

- **Location**: Narrow down groups based on geographic area. This is particularly useful for local communities, events, or city-specific groups.

- **Activity Level**: Some groups are highly active, while others may be inactive. Check for indicators such as "3 posts a day" or "Inactive."

- **Group Type**: If you're looking for a specific type of group (e.g., Buy and Sell groups, Support groups), you can filter by category.

- **Membership Requirements**: Some groups may ask for answers to questions or specific criteria to join.

4. Browsing Suggested Groups

Facebook's algorithm often recommends groups based on your profile activity, likes, and current group memberships. To find these suggestions:

- Navigate to the Groups section on the left sidebar (on desktop) or the Groups tab on the mobile app.

- Scroll down to "Suggested for You."

- Browse through the list and click on groups that catch your interest.

5. Reading Group Descriptions

Before requesting to join a group, take the time to read its description. The description will typically outline the group's purpose, rules, and what members can expect. Pay attention to the following:

- **Topics Covered:** Does the group align with your interests?

- **Rules and Etiquette:** Ensure you are comfortable with the rules. For example, some groups prohibit self-promotion or certain types of posts.

- **Membership Requirements:** Some groups may require you to answer questions, agree to rules, or meet specific criteria before approval.

6. Checking Group Activity

An active group is often more valuable than one with little engagement. To assess activity levels:

- Look at the number of posts per day or week.

- Check how recent the last post was.

- Consider the number of members actively engaging (likes, comments, etc.).

Groups with consistent activity are more likely to provide meaningful discussions and connections.

Best Practices for Choosing Groups

To make the most of your Facebook Group experience, keep the following tips in mind:

- **Join Groups with Clear Moderation:** Well-moderated groups tend to be more organized and free from spam or irrelevant posts.

- **Look for Niche Communities:** Larger groups may feel overwhelming. Sometimes smaller, niche groups offer a more intimate and supportive environment.

- **Avoid Overcommitting:** Start by joining a few groups and engaging meaningfully before adding more.

Exploring Groups Beyond Search

1. Recommendations from Friends

Your Facebook friends may already be part of groups that align with your interests. Browse through their profiles or ask for suggestions directly.

2. Discovering Groups Through Pages

If you follow a Page that shares your interests, it may link to related groups. For instance, a local yoga studio's Page might have a Facebook Group for its community.

3. External Communities

Sometimes, external websites, forums, or real-world communities provide links to their Facebook Groups. Searching through blogs, Reddit threads, or newsletters may reveal hidden gems.

Next Steps After Finding Groups

Once you've found groups you're interested in, the next steps involve joining and participating effectively. In the upcoming sections, we'll cover how to engage with group content, make meaningful contributions, and even create your own group if needed.

By investing time in finding the right Facebook Groups, you'll unlock a world of opportunities to connect, learn, and grow within your chosen communities.

3.2.2 Engaging with Group Content

Engaging with group content is one of the most rewarding aspects of Facebook. Groups are spaces where people come together to share their thoughts, ask questions, and build connections over shared interests. Whether it's a local community group, a professional network, or a fan club, knowing how to effectively interact with group content is key to maximizing the value of your experience. Here's a comprehensive guide to help you engage with group content effectively and meaningfully.

Understanding Group Dynamics

Before engaging with content, it's important to understand the group's purpose and dynamics.

- **Read the Group Description:** The group description usually outlines the purpose, target audience, and guidelines for interaction. Take a moment to review this to ensure your contributions align with the group's intent.

- **Observe Before Posting:** If you're new to a group, spend some time observing the type of posts and interactions. This will help you understand the tone and expectations of the group.

- **Follow Group Rules:** Most groups have specific rules regarding behavior, language, and content. Always adhere to these rules to avoid conflicts or removal from the group.

Types of Group Content to Engage With

Facebook groups typically host a variety of content types. Engaging with each type effectively requires a slightly different approach.

1. **Posts and Discussions:**

    o **Reacting to Posts:** Use Facebook's reaction buttons (Like, Love, Haha, etc.) to show your response to posts. Reactions are a quick and easy way to participate without typing a comment.

    o **Commenting Thoughtfully:** When commenting on posts, ensure your comments are respectful, relevant, and add value. For instance, if someone is asking for advice, provide constructive and helpful input.

    o **Asking Questions:** If you need clarification or want to learn more about a post, asking questions is a great way to engage. For example, "This is interesting! Could you explain a bit more about how this works?"

2. **Polls and Surveys:**

    o Many groups use polls to gather opinions or make decisions. Participate in these by selecting the option that best represents your view.

    o If you feel comfortable, share a comment explaining your choice. This can lead to deeper discussions.

3. **Live Videos and Events:**

- o **Join Live Streams:** Many groups host live streams to discuss topics or hold Q&A sessions. Actively participate by asking questions in the comment section or sharing your thoughts on the discussion.

- o **RSVP to Events:** If a group organizes virtual or in-person events, consider attending. This allows you to build stronger connections and engage in real-time discussions.

4. **Shared Resources:**

- o Groups often share resources like articles, guides, or videos. Take the time to review these and comment on what you found helpful or share additional insights.

- o If you have relevant resources, you can also share them, provided it aligns with group rules.

Best Practices for Engaging with Group Content

1. **Be Respectful and Inclusive:** Always approach discussions with an open mind and a respectful tone. Avoid personal attacks, controversial comments, or divisive topics unless the group explicitly encourages debates.

2. **Stay Relevant:** When commenting or posting, ensure your contributions align with the group's purpose. For example, in a group about photography, focus on topics like techniques, equipment, or experiences, rather than unrelated content.

3. **Engage Consistently:** Regular participation helps you become a recognized and trusted member of the group. Aim to contribute at least a few times a week by commenting, reacting to posts, or sharing valuable content.

4. **Use Clear Communication:**

- o Keep your comments concise and to the point.

- o Use proper grammar and avoid excessive use of emojis or slang, especially in professional groups.

5. **Be Supportive:** Many people join groups seeking help or advice. Offering encouragement or practical solutions fosters a positive environment and helps build strong connections.

Tips for Writing Your Own Posts in Groups

Engagement is a two-way street. If you want people to engage with your posts, ensure they are well-crafted and inviting.

1. **Choose a Clear Topic:** Select topics that are relevant to the group. For instance, in a cooking group, you could share a recipe, ask for tips, or post about your cooking experiences.

2. **Write an Engaging Caption:**

   o   Start with a hook to grab attention.

   o   Include a call to action, such as "What do you think?" or "Has anyone else tried this?"

3. **Add Visuals:** Posts with photos or videos tend to get more engagement. For example, sharing a picture of a finished dish in a food group or a screenshot of a problem in a tech group can spark discussions.

4. **Tag Members or Admins (When Appropriate):** If someone in the group has expertise related to your post, tagging them can encourage them to contribute. However, avoid over-tagging as it can come across as spammy.

Handling Negative Interactions

1. **Ignore Trolls:** If someone posts inflammatory or irrelevant comments, it's often best to ignore them. Engaging with trolls can escalate conflicts.

2. **Report Problematic Content:** Use Facebook's reporting tools to notify group admins about posts or comments that violate group rules or Facebook's community standards.

3. **Stay Calm and Professional:** If you find yourself in a disagreement, approach it with a calm and rational mindset. Avoid escalating the situation.

Benefits of Active Engagement

1. **Build Relationships:** Regular interaction helps you form connections with like-minded people, whether for personal growth or professional networking.

2. **Gain Knowledge:** Groups are a treasure trove of information. Engaging with content allows you to learn from others' experiences and insights.

3. **Establish Your Presence:** Active participation can position you as a valuable member of the community, which might lead to collaboration opportunities or recognition.

4. **Contribute to a Positive Community:** By engaging thoughtfully, you contribute to a supportive and thriving environment that benefits all members.

Conclusion

Engaging with group content on Facebook is more than just reacting to posts or leaving a comment. It's about building meaningful connections, contributing value, and making the most out of the group experience. By following these tips and best practices, you'll not only enhance your own experience but also play a vital role in fostering a vibrant and collaborative community.

3.2.3 Creating Your Own Group

Creating your own Facebook group can be an excellent way to build a community, share ideas, and connect with like-minded people. Whether you're starting a group for a hobby, business, or cause, the process is straightforward. Below, we'll guide you step-by-step through the process of creating and managing a Facebook group successfully.

Step 1: Why Create a Facebook Group?

Before diving into the technical steps, it's essential to understand the purpose of your group. Ask yourself these questions:

- What is the goal of this group? (For example, to share information, provide support, organize events, or promote a business.)

- Who is your target audience? (Are they hobbyists, customers, friends, or colleagues?)

- What type of content will you share? (Discussions, resources, images, videos, etc.)

- How active will the group be?(Daily interactions, occasional updates, or long-term projects?)

Having a clear vision will help you design and manage your group effectively.

Step 2: Creating a Facebook Group

Here's how to create a Facebook group step-by-step:

1. **Log In to Your Account:** Make sure you're logged into your Facebook account. Groups are tied to individual profiles or pages.

2. **Navigate to the Groups Section:**

   o On desktop: Click the **"Groups"** option in the left-hand menu.

   o On mobile: Tap the three horizontal lines (menu) in the top right corner, then select **"Groups"**.

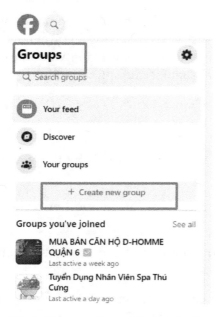

3. **Click "Create Group":** On the Groups page, find and click the **"Create New Group"** button (usually located at the top right on desktop or in the Groups section on mobile).

4. **Name Your Group:**

   o Choose a name that reflects the group's purpose.

   o Keep it short, clear, and specific (e.g., "Baking Enthusiasts of New York" or "Freelance Writers Network").

5. **Choose Privacy Settings:** Facebook offers three main privacy options:

   o **Public Group:** Anyone can find and join.

   o **Private Group:** Only invited members can see the group content.

   o **Hidden Group:** Even more exclusive, this option makes the group unsearchable.

For most cases, **Private** is the best choice if you want to build a safe and focused community.

6. **Invite Initial Members:**

   o Start with close friends, colleagues, or those you think will benefit from the group.

   o You can skip this step initially and add members later.

7. **Customize Your Group Settings:** Once the group is created, take time to personalize it:

   o Add a group cover photo that represents your community.

   o Write a group description detailing the purpose and rules of the group.

   o Create a welcoming pinned post to greet new members.

Step 3: Managing Group Settings

Facebook allows you to customize the group further through settings:

1. **Group Rules:** Define clear rules for your group. For example:

    o   Be respectful to others.

    o   No spam or self-promotion.

    o   Stay on-topic.

2. **Approval Settings:**

    o   **Membership Requests:** Decide if members can join automatically or require admin approval.

    o   **Post Approval:** Choose whether posts need to be approved by admins before they appear in the group.

3. **Group Features:** Explore additional features:

    o   Polls to gather opinions.

    o   Events to schedule group meetups or activities.

    o   Guides to organize resources for learning.

Step 4: Engaging with Your Group

Once your group is live, you'll need to keep it active and engaging. Here's how:

1. **Regular Posts:** Share relevant content frequently. Ideas include:

    o   Questions to spark discussions.

    o   Tutorials, videos, or articles.

    o   Personal stories or experiences.

2. **Respond to Members:** Acknowledge comments and interact with members to make them feel valued.

3. **Encourage Contributions:** Motivate members to share their thoughts, post content, or ask questions. You can even highlight the most active contributors.

4. **Host Events or Live Sessions:** Use Facebook Live to host Q&A sessions, tutorials, or webinars.

5. **Moderate the Group:** Monitor posts and comments to ensure they align with the rules. Use tools to mute or remove disruptive members if needed.

Step 5: Growing Your Group

To expand your group, consider these strategies:

1. **Promote Your Group:**

   o Share your group link on your Facebook profile or other social media platforms.

   o Collaborate with similar groups or pages to cross-promote.

2. **Optimize Group Discoverability:**

   o Use keywords in your group name and description to help people find it.

   o Add tags that represent your group's focus.

3. **Encourage Member Invites:** Ask your members to invite friends or colleagues who may benefit from the group.

Step 6: Handling Challenges

Managing a Facebook group can come with challenges. Here's how to address some common issues:

1. **Dealing with Spam:**

   o Remove posts that violate the rules.

   o Use membership screening questions to filter out bots.

2. **Conflict Resolution:**

   o Stay neutral in disputes and enforce rules fairly.

   o Use direct messages to address sensitive issues with members.

3. **Inactive Members:**

   o Encourage re-engagement with surveys or special events.

    o   Consider removing inactive members periodically.

Step 7: Measuring Your Group's Success

Facebook offers insights for group admins to monitor engagement. Use these tools to evaluate performance:

1. **Member Growth:** Track how many new members are joining weekly or monthly.

2. **Engagement Metrics:** Analyze the number of posts, comments, and reactions to see what content resonates most with your members.

3. **Feedback:**
   Conduct polls or surveys to understand what members want from the group.

Conclusion

Creating a Facebook group is more than just setting up a digital space—it's about building a thriving community. With thoughtful planning, regular engagement, and effective management, your group can become a hub for meaningful interactions and shared experiences. Follow the steps above, and you'll be well on your way to unlocking the full potential of your Facebook group!

3.3 Following Pages and Influencers

3.3.1 Liking and Following Pages

Facebook Pages are one of the most effective ways to stay connected with your favorite brands, influencers, celebrities, businesses, and organizations. Whether you're a casual user looking to follow updates or a professional seeking insights from industry leaders, liking and following Pages can help you personalize your Facebook experience. This section will guide you through the process of finding, liking, and following Pages, while also explaining the benefits of doing so. We'll also explore tips for organizing the Pages you follow to optimize your News Feed.

What Are Facebook Pages?

Facebook Pages are public profiles designed for businesses, organizations, public figures, and content creators to share information, interact with their audience, and build a community. Unlike personal profiles, Pages can be followed without sending a friend request, making them an open platform for content sharing. Here are some key features of Facebook Pages:

- **Public Access:** Anyone on Facebook can like or follow a Page to receive updates.

- **Specialized Content:** Pages share posts, videos, events, and promotions tailored to their audience.

- **Engagement Tools:** Pages allow users to like, comment, and share content, as well as participate in polls, contests, and discussions.

Why Like and Follow Pages?

Liking and following Pages provide a variety of benefits, depending on your goals and interests. Here are some reasons to engage with Facebook Pages:

1. **Stay Updated:** Receive timely updates from your favorite brands, influencers, or organizations.

2. **Discover New Content:** Explore new ideas, products, or services related to your interests.

3. **Support Businesses and Creators:** Show appreciation and help Pages grow by engaging with their content.

4. **Network and Learn:** Follow Pages in your professional field to gain insights, tips, and resources.

5. **Event Notifications:** Stay informed about upcoming events, webinars, or product launches.

Step-by-Step Guide to Liking and Following Pages

Step 1: Finding a Facebook Page

Before you can like or follow a Page, you need to find it. There are several ways to search for Pages on Facebook:

1. **Using the Search Bar:**

   o Type the name of the brand, celebrity, or topic you're interested in into the search bar at the top of the Facebook interface.

   o Click on the "Pages" tab in the search results to filter out personal profiles and groups.

   o Browse the list of results until you find the Page you're looking for.

2. **Browsing Recommendations:**

   o Visit the "Explore" section on the left-hand side of your home screen and click on "Pages."

   o Facebook will recommend Pages based on your interests, interactions, and friends' activity.

3. **From Shared Content:**

   o If you see a post shared by a friend or another Page, you can click on the Page's name at the top of the post to visit their profile.

Step 2: Liking a Page

Once you've found a Page you're interested in, you can like it to show your support and begin receiving updates:

1. Click the **"Like"** button located below the Page's cover photo.

2. After liking the Page, the button will change to **"Liked"**, indicating that you've successfully liked it.

Step 3: Following a Page

Liking a Page automatically subscribes you to follow it, but you can choose to follow without liking if you prefer:

1. Click the **"Follow"** button on the Page's profile.

2. You can customize your follow settings by clicking the **"..." (More Options)** button and selecting **"Follow Settings."** Here, you can:

    o Prioritize posts from the Page in your News Feed.

○ Turn on or off notifications for posts, videos, or live streams.

Tips for Managing the Pages You Follow

Once you start liking and following multiple Pages, it's important to manage them to avoid an overwhelming News Feed. Here's how:

1. **Organize Pages into Favorites:**

   ○ Go to your "Follow Settings" and select "Favorites" to ensure posts from specific Pages are prioritized in your feed.

   ○ You can add up to 30 Pages to your Favorites list.

2. **Unfollow or Unlike Inactive Pages:**

   ○ Periodically review the Pages you follow by going to the "Pages" section in your profile.

   ○ Unfollow Pages that no longer interest you to declutter your feed.

3. **Adjust Notification Settings:**

- Visit the Page's profile and click on "Follow Settings" to manage how often you're notified about new content.

4. **Use Saved Posts:**

  - If you find valuable content from a Page but don't want to keep scrolling through the feed to find it later, use the "Save Post" option.

Common Mistakes to Avoid When Following Pages

1. **Liking Too Many Pages at Once:** Following too many Pages can flood your News Feed, making it harder to focus on the content that matters most to you.

2. **Ignoring Privacy Settings:** Be cautious when engaging with Pages. Avoid sharing personal information in comments or messages unless you trust the Page's authenticity.

3. **Following Fake or Spam Pages:** Verify the legitimacy of a Page before following it by checking for a blue verification badge or browsing through its content.

Best Practices for Liking and Following Pages

- **Engage Regularly:** Interact with posts by liking, commenting, or sharing to stay connected.

- **Support Local Businesses:** Follow Pages of local shops, restaurants, and organizations to stay informed about your community.

- **Be Selective:** Focus on Pages that align with your interests, values, or professional goals.

- **Discover Niche Communities:** Explore lesser-known Pages to find unique content and connect with like-minded individuals.

By following these steps and tips, you'll be able to build a more meaningful and tailored Facebook experience. Liking and following Pages is not just about receiving updates—it's a way to connect, learn, and grow in both personal and professional spheres. In the next section, we'll explore how to interact with the content shared by Pages and influencers to maximize your engagement.

3.3.2 Interacting with Page Content

Interacting with page content on Facebook is one of the best ways to stay engaged with the pages you follow, discover valuable information, and build connections within your community. Whether you're following businesses, celebrities, influencers, or organizations, engaging with their content allows you to contribute to discussions, show support, and get the most out of your Facebook experience. Below is a step-by-step guide on how to interact with page content effectively and make your interactions meaningful.

Understanding the Basics of Page Content

Pages on Facebook regularly post various types of content, including text updates, photos, videos, links, polls, and live streams. Each type of content offers unique ways to engage. Here are the most common types of content you'll encounter:

- **Text Updates:** These are simple posts where pages share news, announcements, or ideas. They're often designed to spark conversation.

- **Photos and Videos:** Visual content is highly engaging and can range from promotional materials to behind-the-scenes glimpses.

- **Links and Articles:** Many pages share external links to blogs, news articles, or their website.

- **Polls and Questions:** These posts encourage interaction and often seek audience opinions.

- **Live Streams:** Pages may go live to host events, Q&A sessions, or tutorials in real-time.

Step-by-Step Guide to Engaging with Page Content

1. Reacting to Posts

Facebook offers a variety of reactions beyond just a "Like." These reactions allow you to express different emotions:

- **Like:** Use this to show general appreciation for the post.

- **Love:** Perfect for posts that resonate deeply or inspire you.

- **Care:** A reaction to show empathy or support.

- **Haha, Wow, Sad, and Angry:** These reactions allow you to express humor, surprise, sadness, or frustration.

To react to a post:

- Hover over or long-press the "Like" button on mobile.

- Select the reaction that best reflects your feelings.

💡 *Tip:* Choose your reactions thoughtfully. Overusing the "Angry" reaction on posts you don't agree with can create unnecessary conflict.

2. Commenting on Posts

Comments are one of the most direct ways to engage with a page's content. You can use the comments section to:

- **Ask questions:** For example, "Can you tell me more about this product?"

- **Share your opinion:** "I love this initiative! Keep up the great work!"

- **Show support:** "Congratulations on this achievement!"

- **Tag friends:** "@[Friend's Name], this reminds me of our trip last year!"

When commenting:

- Keep your tone positive and respectful.

- Avoid spamming or posting irrelevant comments.

- Add value to the conversation by sharing your thoughts or experiences.

💡 *Tip:* Engaging with comments made by others can also help you connect with like-minded individuals.

3. Sharing Posts

Sharing is a powerful way to amplify content you find valuable or interesting. When you share a post, it appears on your timeline and can be seen by your friends or followers.

To share a post:

- Click the "Share" button below the post.

- Choose between:

    o **Share Now (Friends):** Immediately shares the post to your timeline.

    o **Write Post:** Adds your personal thoughts before sharing.

    o **Share to a Group:** Posts the content in a group you're part of.

    o **Send as Message:** Shares privately via Messenger.

💡 *Tip:* When sharing, include a short comment explaining why you think the post is worth sharing.

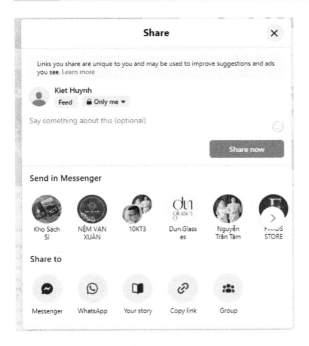

4. Engaging with Stories

Many pages use Facebook Stories to share time-sensitive updates. These stories appear at the top of your feed and disappear after 24 hours.

To interact with stories:

- **React:** Tap on the story and use reactions to express your thoughts.
- **Reply:** Swipe up on the story to send a private message to the page.
- **Share:** Some stories allow you to share them with others.

💡 *Tip:* Stories often include polls, quizzes, or clickable links. Participate actively for a more engaging experience.

5. Watching and Interacting with Live Videos

Live videos are an interactive way for pages to engage with their audience in real-time.

To interact with live videos:

- **React in Real Time:** Tap reactions to show your emotions as the video progresses.

- **Comment Live:** Ask questions or share your thoughts in the live chat.

- **Share the Live Stream:** Encourage others to join by sharing the live video on your timeline.

💡 *Tip:* If you miss a live video, most pages save them so you can watch and comment later.

6. Participating in Polls and Q&A Posts

Many pages use polls or Q&A posts to interact with their followers and gather opinions.

- **For Polls:** Simply click on the option that best represents your view.

- **For Q&A Posts:** Write your questions or vote for others' questions.

💡 *Tip:* Engaging with polls can also help pages tailor their content to your interests.

Best Practices for Interacting with Page Content

1. **Be Respectful:** Always maintain a positive and respectful tone, even when you disagree.

2. **Avoid Over-Engagement:** Don't spam comments or reactions; this can be seen as insincere.

3. **Add Value:** Your engagement should contribute to the conversation.

4. **Check Notifications:** Enable notifications for pages you follow to stay updated on their posts.

5. **Report Issues:** If you see inappropriate or harmful content, use the "Report" option to notify Facebook.

Leveraging Interactions for Personal Growth

Interacting with page content isn't just about engagement—it's also a way to grow personally and professionally:

- **Networking Opportunities:** Commenting on niche-specific pages can help you connect with like-minded individuals.

- **Learning New Skills:** Many educational and professional pages share valuable tips and resources.

- **Staying Informed:** Follow news pages, industry leaders, or local organizations to stay updated.

Conclusion

Interacting with page content on Facebook is a key part of making the platform a dynamic and rewarding space. By reacting, commenting, sharing, and participating in the various content formats available, you not only support the pages you love but also enrich your own Facebook experience. Remember, meaningful engagement builds stronger connections and makes your presence on the platform more impactful.

CHAPTER III
Sharing Content on Facebook

4.1 Creating Posts

Sharing content on Facebook is at the core of connecting with friends, family, and communities. A well-crafted post can spark engaging conversations, share important updates, or entertain your audience. In this section, we'll delve into the process of creating posts on Facebook, starting with one of the most basic yet versatile types: **text posts**.

4.1.1 Text Posts

A **text post** is the simplest form of content you can share on Facebook. Despite its simplicity, it's a powerful tool for communication and interaction. A text post allows you to express thoughts, ask questions, share updates, and engage with your audience without needing additional elements like images or videos. Below, we'll explore how to create an effective text post and maximize its impact.

What is a Text Post?

A text post on Facebook is simply a message consisting of words, without any accompanying media such as images, videos, or links. It is often used for announcements, short updates, personal thoughts, or starting conversations. Text posts can be enhanced with features like emojis, hashtags, or mentions to make them more engaging.

Why Use Text Posts?

Text posts are ideal for:

- **Quick Updates**: Sharing news, thoughts, or information without needing visual elements.

- **Starting Conversations**: Asking open-ended questions or seeking opinions from your audience.

- **Accessibility**: Text posts load faster than posts with heavy media, making them accessible even on slow internet connections.

- **Personal Touch**: Text-only posts often feel more direct and conversational, which can foster a stronger sense of connection.

How to Create a Text Post

Step 1: Open the Facebook App or Website

1. Log in to your Facebook account.

2. On the home page or your profile page, locate the **"What's on your mind?"** box at the top of the feed.

Step 2: Start Typing Your Message

1. Click inside the text box.

2. Type your message. This can be anything from a personal update to a question you want to ask your friends.

Step 3: Enhance Your Post (Optional)

To make your text post stand out, you can:

- **Use Emojis**: Emojis can help convey tone or add personality to your post. For example, instead of saying "I'm excited," you can write "I'm excited 🎉!"

- **Add Hashtags**: Hashtags categorize your post, making it easier for others to find. For instance, a post about fitness might include hashtags like #FitnessJourney or #HealthyLiving.

- **Mention Friends**: Use the @ symbol followed by a friend's name to tag them in your post. This draws their attention to your content and increases engagement.

- **Use Bold or Colored Text**: On mobile, Facebook often suggests colorful backgrounds or formatting options to make your post visually appealing.

Step 4: Choose Your Audience

Before publishing, decide who will see your post. Click on the audience selector (usually showing "Public," "Friends," or "Only Me") and choose your desired setting. You can share it with:

- **Public**: Anyone on Facebook, even those who are not your friends.

- **Friends**: Only people on your friends list.

- **Friends Except...**: Exclude specific individuals from seeing your post.

- **Only Me**: Keep the post private for personal notes or records.

Step 5: Post Your Content

1. Once you're happy with your text post, click **Post** (or **Share** on mobile).

2. Your text post will now appear on your timeline and in the news feeds of those in your chosen audience.

Best Practices for Text Posts

1. Keep It Concise and Clear

Long paragraphs can be overwhelming, especially for casual readers scrolling through their feeds. Aim for short, punchy sentences that quickly convey your message.

2. Use a Conversational Tone

Writing as if you're talking to a friend makes your post more relatable. Avoid overly formal language unless the context requires it.

3. Add a Call-to-Action (CTA)

Encourage engagement by ending your post with a question or prompt. For example:

- "What do you think about this idea?"
- "Share your tips in the comments below!"

4. Avoid Overloading with Emojis or Hashtags

While emojis and hashtags can enhance a post, overusing them can make it look cluttered. Stick to 1–3 hashtags and a handful of emojis that complement your message.

5. Proofread Before Posting

Grammar and spelling errors can undermine your message's clarity. Take a moment to review your post before clicking "Share."

Advanced Tips for Engaging Text Posts

1. Share Personal Stories

People love stories. Sharing a brief, personal anecdote can make your post more relatable and human. For example:

- "I finally completed my first marathon today! It was tough, but the feeling at the finish line was worth it."

2. Spark Debate or Discussion

Post thought-provoking statements or questions to invite comments. For example:

- "Do you think social media is helping or harming communication? Let's discuss!"

3. Use Quotes or Insights

Inspirational or thought-provoking quotes resonate with many people. For instance:

- "'Success is not final; failure is not fatal: It is the courage to continue that counts.' – Winston Churchill."

4. Leverage Trends

Posting about trending topics can boost engagement. Ensure your post is relevant and adds value to the discussion.

Analyzing Engagement

After posting, pay attention to how your audience responds:

- **Likes and Reactions**: Gauge how your message resonates.

- **Comments**: Engage with people who take the time to reply. Responding to comments can boost visibility and strengthen relationships.

- **Shares**: If people share your post, it indicates strong resonance or relatability.

Common Mistakes to Avoid with Text Posts

1. Being Too Vague

Ambiguous posts can confuse your audience. Be specific about your message or intention.

2. Posting Without Context

Ensure your post has enough background for your audience to understand it, especially if it's related to an ongoing event or personal experience.

3. Overposting

Flooding your audience's feed with frequent posts can lead to disengagement. Post intentionally and at strategic times.

4. Ignoring Feedback

Failing to respond to comments or reactions can make your audience feel undervalued. Always engage with your audience when possible.

Conclusion

Creating effective text posts on Facebook is an art and a science. By following these steps and best practices, you can craft posts that resonate with your audience, spark meaningful interactions, and elevate your presence on the platform. Whether you're sharing a quick update or starting a deep conversation, a well-thought-out text post is a valuable tool for communication.

4.1.2 Photo and Video Posts

Sharing photos and videos on Facebook is one of the most engaging ways to connect with your audience. Whether you want to share a personal moment, showcase a product, or simply entertain, visual content captures attention more effectively than plain text. This section will guide you through every aspect of creating, editing, and sharing photo and video posts on Facebook.

Why Share Photos and Videos on Facebook?

Before diving into the "how-to," it's essential to understand why photos and videos are vital on Facebook:

1. **Higher Engagement**: Posts with visuals receive significantly more likes, comments, and shares than text-only posts.

2. **Storytelling**: Photos and videos allow you to share stories in a visually compelling way, making your content memorable.

3. **Universal Appeal**: Visual content transcends language barriers and can be enjoyed by anyone.

4. **Showcase Creativity**: With Facebook's tools, you can create eye-catching content that reflects your personality or brand identity.

Step-by-Step Guide to Posting Photos and Videos

1. Preparing Your Photos and Videos

Before you upload anything, ensure your files are ready. Here's what to consider:

- **Resolution**: Use high-quality images (minimum 720p for videos and at least 1200 x 630 pixels for photos).

- **File Format**: Facebook supports popular formats such as JPEG, PNG, MP4, and MOV.

- **Length (for videos)**: Keep videos under 120 minutes and under 4GB in file size. However, shorter videos (1-3 minutes) often perform better for engagement.

- **Orientation**: Use landscape or portrait mode depending on how you want your audience to view the content.

2. Uploading Photos and Videos to Facebook

Step 1: Log in to your account and go to your homepage or timeline.
Step 2: Click the **"What's on your mind?"** text box at the top of your News Feed.
Step 3: Select **"Photo/Video"** from the post options. A file upload window will appear.
Step 4: Choose the photos or videos you want to upload from your device.

- To upload multiple photos, hold down the Ctrl key (Windows) or Command key (Mac) while selecting files.

- For videos, you can upload multiple clips to create a single video post.

3. Customizing Your Post

Once you've selected your photos or videos, Facebook allows you to personalize your post:

- **Add a Caption**: Write a description that complements your content. A good caption is clear, concise, and encourages interaction. For example, "What's your favorite way to spend a Sunday afternoon? ☐ #RelaxAndRecharge."

- **Tag People**: Click the "Tag Friends" icon to tag people in your post. This is great for sharing group photos or moments with others.

- **Location**: Add a location to let your audience know where the photo or video was taken.

- **Feelings/Activities**: Add how you're feeling or what you're doing for a more personal touch (e.g., "Feeling excited 🎉").

4. Enhancing Your Photos and Videos

Facebook provides basic tools to enhance your visuals:

- **Filters**: Apply filters to improve the appearance of your photos. For example, you can make them brighter, add a vintage effect, or adjust saturation.

- **Crop and Rotate**: Edit your photos directly on Facebook to adjust framing or orientation.

- **Video Trimming**: For videos, you can trim the beginning or end to remove unnecessary footage.

Tips for Effective Photo and Video Posts

To maximize the impact of your posts, follow these best practices:

1. Use Eye-Catching Visuals

- **Lighting**: Ensure your photos and videos are well-lit, whether you're shooting indoors or outdoors.

- **Composition**: Follow the rule of thirds to create balanced, professional-looking visuals.

- **Focus**: Avoid blurry photos or shaky videos. Use a tripod or stabilizer for steady shots.

2. Tell a Story

- Create a narrative with your visuals. For instance, a vacation photo album could include a mix of landscapes, food, and candid moments to give your audience a sense of the experience.

3. Keep Videos Short and Engaging

- Start with a strong hook in the first 3 seconds to grab attention.

- Use captions or subtitles for videos, as many users watch without sound.

- Include a call-to-action (CTA) like "Share this video if you agree!" or "Comment your thoughts below."

4. Post at Optimal Times

- Analyze when your audience is most active using Facebook Insights. Generally, early mornings and evenings see higher engagement rates.

Privacy Settings for Photo and Video Posts

When sharing content, it's important to consider who can view it:

- **Public**: Visible to anyone, including people not on your friends list.

- **Friends Only**: Shared with only your Facebook friends.

- **Specific Friends**: Choose certain people to share with while excluding others.

- **Only Me**: For private content visible only to you.

You can adjust these settings by clicking the audience selector (globe, friends icon, or lock symbol) before posting.

Special Features for Photos and Videos

Facebook offers unique features to enhance your posts:

1. Photo Albums

- Organize multiple photos into albums, such as "Family Vacation 2025" or "My Artwork."

- Albums allow you to keep related content together and make it easier for viewers to browse.

2. Facebook Stories

- Share photos and videos that disappear after 24 hours. Use Stories for quick updates or behind-the-scenes glimpses.

3. Slideshow and Carousel Posts

- Create a slideshow from multiple photos or share a carousel of images and videos in one post. These formats are great for storytelling or showcasing products.

4. Live Videos

- Use Facebook Live to broadcast real-time video to your audience. Live videos are highly engaging and allow viewers to comment as they watch.

Common Mistakes to Avoid

To ensure your photo and video posts perform well, steer clear of these pitfalls:

1. **Overposting**: Avoid bombarding your audience with too many visuals in a short period. Quality over quantity!

2. **Ignoring Engagement**: Respond to comments and messages to build a connection with your audience.

3. **Using Poor Quality Visuals**: Low-resolution images or videos can harm your credibility.

Conclusion

Sharing photos and videos on Facebook is more than just uploading files; it's about creating content that resonates with your audience. By following these detailed steps and tips, you can make your photo and video posts stand out, engage more effectively, and truly unlock the power of visual storytelling.

4.1.3 Adding Emojis and Tags

Adding emojis and tags to your Facebook posts can significantly enhance engagement and visibility. Emojis add personality and emotional context, while tags help connect your post to other users, pages, or locations. In this section, we'll guide you through the process of using emojis and tags effectively, explain why they matter, and share practical tips to optimize their use.

Understanding Emojis: Why They Matter

Emojis are small visual icons that represent emotions, objects, and ideas. When used in Facebook posts, they help convey tone, mood, and intention that might be difficult to express through text alone. Emojis also make posts more engaging, colorful, and appealing to users who quickly scroll through their feeds.

Benefits of Using Emojis in Facebook Posts

- **Visual Appeal**: Emojis draw attention to your post, making it stand out in a crowded feed.

- **Emotional Connection**: They help your audience understand the sentiment behind your words, whether it's excitement, humor, or empathy.

- **Improved Engagement**: Posts with emojis often receive higher engagement rates, as they feel more personal and relatable.

- **Universal Language**: Emojis transcend language barriers and communicate meaning across cultures.

How to Add Emojis to Your Facebook Posts

Step 1: Open the Post Editor

- On the Facebook homepage, click on the "What's on your mind?" text box to start a new post.

Step 2: Access the Emoji Keyboard

- **On Desktop**: Use your computer's emoji keyboard by right-clicking in the text box and selecting "Emoji" (on Mac, use Control + Command + Space; on Windows, press Windows Key + . or Windows Key + ;).

- **On Mobile**: Tap the emoji icon on your keyboard to open the emoji selection screen.

Step 3: Choose Relevant Emojis

- Browse through the categories (e.g., smileys, animals, objects) to find emojis that match the tone or topic of your post.

- Avoid overusing emojis—select 1–3 that complement your text without overwhelming it.

Step 4: Insert Emojis in the Text

- Click or tap the emoji you want to add, and it will appear in your post.

- You can mix emojis with text naturally to make your message flow smoothly.

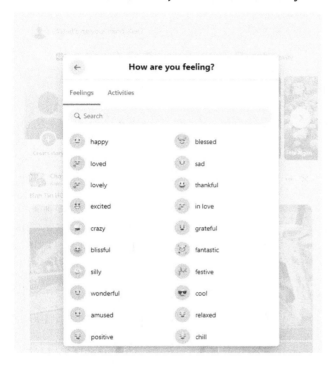

Best Practices for Using Emojis

1. **Match the Tone of Your Post**: Ensure the emojis align with the mood of your content. For instance:

   o Use 🎉, □, or ✨ for celebratory posts.

   o Use ♥□, ☺, or ❀ for positive and heartfelt messages.

   o Avoid using conflicting emojis that might confuse readers.

2. **Keep It Simple**: Don't overuse emojis; they should enhance your message, not dominate it. For example:

- o Overused: "I'm so happy today!!! ☺☺☺🎉🎉🎉🎉✨✨✨"
- o Balanced: "I'm so happy today! ☺🎉✨"

3. **Use Emojis to Replace Words (When Appropriate)**: In some cases, emojis can replace words for a creative twist. For example:

   - o "I ❤□ coffee ☕ every morning."
   - o "Who's ready for the weekend? □□🍹✨"

4. **Consider Your Audience**: Emojis are fun and engaging, but they might not suit every audience. For professional updates, use emojis sparingly or skip them altogether.

Using Tags in Facebook Posts

Tags are a powerful tool for connecting your posts to specific people, pages, or locations. By tagging, you notify the tagged entity, encourage interaction, and expand the reach of your content.

Types of Tags You Can Use

1. **Tagging People**: Mention friends or colleagues in your post to involve them in the conversation.

2. **Tagging Pages**: Highlight brands, businesses, or public figures by tagging their official Facebook pages.

3. **Tagging Locations**: Add a location tag to share where you are or to promote a specific venue.

How to Tag in Facebook Posts

Step 1: Start Writing Your Post

- Begin by typing your message in the text box on the Facebook post editor.

Step 2: Use the "@" Symbol for Tagging People or Pages

- To tag someone or a page, type the "@" symbol followed by their name. For example, "@John Smith" or "@Starbucks".

- A dropdown menu will appear with matching names. Select the correct one to create the tag.

Step 3: Add a Location Tag (Optional)

- Below the text box, click on the "Check In" icon (a red pin) to add a location.

- Search for the location you want to tag, then select it from the list.

Step 4: Review Your Tags

- Make sure all tags are correct and relevant before posting.

Best Practices for Using Tags

1. **Be Selective**: Only tag people or pages directly related to your post. Irrelevant tags can annoy others and reduce your credibility.

2. **Seek Permission**: Before tagging friends or colleagues, ensure they are comfortable being mentioned in your post.

3. **Use Tags Strategically**

   o Tag a business page to show support or build a partnership.

   o Mention key individuals to encourage responses or shares.

4. **Avoid Over-Tagging**: Overloading your post with tags can look spammy and may deter engagement.

Combining Emojis and Tags Effectively

When used together, emojis and tags can create a highly engaging post. For example:

- **Personal Post**: "Had an amazing dinner with @Sarah at ☐ Taco Palace in NYC! Highly recommend this spot! 🍴✨ #Foodie"

- **Business Post**: "Excited to announce our partnership with @TechCo! 🚀 Stay tuned for exciting updates. #Innovation #Collaboration"

- **Event Post**: "We're thrilled to host the Annual Charity Gala at @GrandHotel ☐☐ on June 15th! Save the date! ♥☐ #GivingBack"

Common Mistakes to Avoid

1. **Overloading Emojis**: Too many emojis can make your post hard to read.

2. **Irrelevant Tags**: Tagging unrelated people or pages can lead to negative feedback.

3. **Misaligned Tone**: Using cheerful emojis in a serious post can send mixed signals.

By adding emojis and tags thoughtfully, you can make your Facebook posts more engaging, relatable, and far-reaching. When used correctly, they help convey emotions, involve others, and enhance your content's appeal.

4.2 Using Stories and Reels

4.2.1 How Stories Work

Facebook Stories have become one of the most dynamic and popular features for sharing moments in a visually engaging and time-sensitive format. This section provides a complete guide to understanding how Stories work, how to create them effectively, and tips for maximizing their potential. Whether you're using Stories for personal connections or promoting a brand, mastering this feature will enhance your Facebook experience.

What Are Facebook Stories?

Facebook Stories are short, visual posts that disappear 24 hours after being shared. These posts can include photos, videos, text, or even interactive elements like polls and stickers. Stories appear at the top of your News Feed and are designed for quick consumption, making them an effective way to share updates, capture attention, and interact with your audience.

Key Characteristics of Stories:

- **Ephemeral Nature:** Stories vanish after 24 hours, encouraging users to post more spontaneous and timely content.

- **Full-Screen Experience:** Stories are displayed in a vertical, full-screen format, making them immersive and engaging.

- **Interactive Features:** Facebook offers tools like stickers, polls, music, and GIFs to make Stories more interactive.

- **Private or Public Sharing:** You can control the audience for your Stories, choosing whether to share with all your friends, a select group, or the public.

Why Use Facebook Stories?

Stories have become an essential tool for personal expression and brand promotion. Here are some of the main reasons why they are so effective:

1. **Reach and Visibility:** Stories are displayed prominently at the top of the app, ensuring they catch the attention of users immediately.

2. **Engagement:** The interactive features of Stories (such as polls and Q&A) encourage direct engagement with viewers.

3. **Timeliness:** Stories are ideal for sharing real-time updates, event highlights, or daily moments.

4. **Authenticity:** Because Stories disappear after 24 hours, they often feel more genuine and less curated than permanent posts.

How to Access Facebook Stories

You can view and create Stories from both the **Facebook app** and **desktop website**.

1. **Viewing Stories:**
   - On the app: Stories are located at the top of your News Feed. Tap a Story to view it.
   - On desktop: Stories appear in the upper-right corner of the Facebook homepage.

2. **Creating Stories:**
   - On the app: Tap on your profile picture in the Stories section and select "Create Story."
   - On desktop: Click "Create a Story" in the Stories section.

Types of Content for Stories

Facebook Stories allow for a variety of content types, making them versatile and creative. Below are the common options you can use:

1. **Photos and Videos:**
   - Capture real-time moments using your camera or upload from your gallery.
   - Videos can be up to **20 seconds long**. For longer videos, Facebook automatically splits them into segments.

2. **Text Stories:**

   o Write text-based updates on customizable backgrounds.

   o Choose different fonts, colors, and alignment to make your message stand out.

3. **Interactive Elements:**

   o Add polls, stickers, or questions to engage your audience.

   o Use sliders or emoji reactions for quick feedback.

4. **Music and Audio:**

   o Include a soundtrack by selecting from Facebook's music library.

   o Add captions to ensure accessibility for all viewers.

5. **Links and Call-to-Actions (For Pages or Verified Profiles):**

   o Pages and verified accounts can include swipe-up links, directing viewers to websites or other content.

Step-by-Step Guide to Creating Stories

Step 1: Open the Stories Creator

- On mobile: Tap your profile picture in the Stories section and select "Create Story."

- On desktop: Click "Create a Story" in the Stories section.

Step 2: Choose Your Content Type

Select whether you want to create a photo, video, or text-based Story. You can either capture new content or upload files from your device.

Step 3: Add Personalization

Use Facebook's tools to customize your Story:

- **Filters:** Swipe to apply visual effects or filters.

- **Text:** Add captions, quotes, or callouts using the text tool.

- **Stickers:** Enhance your Story with stickers like emojis, weather updates, or location tags.

- **Music:** Choose a song to play in the background.

Step 4: Adjust Privacy Settings

Before posting, select who can view your Story:

- **Public:** Anyone on Facebook can see it.

- **Friends Only:** Only your Facebook friends can view your Story.

- **Custom:** Share your Story with a specific group of people.

Step 5: Post Your Story

Once you're satisfied, click "Share" to publish your Story. It will remain visible for 24 hours unless you delete it earlier.

Tips for Creating Engaging Stories

1. **Keep It Short and Simple:** Stories are meant to be consumed quickly. Focus on delivering a clear and concise message.

2. **Use Visual Appeal:** Bright colors, high-quality photos, and engaging videos grab attention.

3. **Add a Call-to-Action (CTA):** Encourage viewers to respond, like, or swipe up for more information.

4. **Post Regularly:** Consistent updates keep your audience engaged and coming back for more.

5. **Experiment with Features:** Try using polls, questions, and stickers to add interactivity to your Stories.

Best Practices for Businesses Using Stories

1. **Show Behind-the-Scenes Content:** Share glimpses of your team, workspace, or daily operations to build authenticity.

2. **Promote Limited-Time Offers:** Use Stories to highlight flash sales or exclusive deals.

3. **Highlight Customer Testimonials:** Share user-generated content to build trust.

4. **Use Analytics:** For business accounts, monitor your Story performance using Facebook Insights.

FAQs About Facebook Stories

Q1: Can I edit a Story after posting it? No, once a Story is published, it cannot be edited. You'll need to delete and repost it if changes are required.

Q2: Can I save my Stories? Yes, Facebook allows you to save Stories to your device or archive them for future reference.

Q3: How can I see who viewed my Story? Open your Story and swipe up to see a list of viewers.

Q4: Are Stories visible to non-Facebook users? No, Stories are only accessible to users logged into Facebook.

By mastering Facebook Stories, you can share content that is both engaging and impactful. Whether you're connecting with friends or growing your audience, Stories provide a creative and interactive way to express yourself. Up next, we'll dive into **Creating and Editing Reels**, another exciting feature to enhance your content creation!

4.2.2 Creating and Editing Reels

Reels are one of Facebook's most engaging and visually captivating features, allowing users to create short, dynamic videos with creative tools like music, filters, text, and effects. Reels are an excellent way to showcase your creativity, share moments, or build your brand. In this section, we'll guide you step-by-step through the process of creating and editing Reels to make the most out of this feature.

What Are Facebook Reels?

Facebook Reels are short videos, typically 15 to 90 seconds long, that allow users to express themselves through quick, engaging content. Unlike regular posts or Stories, Reels are designed to be highly shareable and discoverable, appearing in the Reels tab, on users' feeds, and in search results.

Step 1: Preparing to Create a Reel

Before you start recording or uploading your Reel, it's important to plan your content. Consider the following:

1. **Purpose:** Why are you creating this Reel? Is it for entertainment, education, promotion, or simply to share a moment?

2. **Audience:** Who are you targeting? Understanding your audience helps you create relevant and engaging content.

3. **Theme:** Decide on a theme or idea for your Reel. Whether it's a tutorial, a dance challenge, or a behind-the-scenes glimpse, having a clear concept will make the process smoother.

4. **Assets:** Gather any photos, videos, music, or props you might need for your Reel.

Step 2: Creating Your Reel

2.1 Accessing the Reels Feature

To begin creating a Reel:

1. Open the Facebook app on your mobile device.

2. Navigate to the Reels section, which you can find:

   o On the home screen under the Reels tab.

   o By tapping the "Create" button and selecting "Reel."

3. Tap the "Create Reel" button to get started.

2.2 Recording a Reel

Facebook offers a user-friendly interface to record your Reel directly in the app. Here's how:

1. **Tap the Record Button:** Once you're in the Reels editor, tap the circular record button to start recording.

2. **Control Timing:** You can choose between multiple recording lengths (15, 30, 60, or 90 seconds). Adjust the timer before you start.

3. **Use Hands-Free Mode:** Tap the timer icon to set up a countdown for hands-free recording. This is particularly useful for scenes where you need to move around or perform an action.

4. **Pause and Resume:** You can pause recording by tapping the record button and resume it at any time. This allows you to create a Reel with multiple scenes.

2.3 Uploading Pre-Recorded Clips

If you already have video clips or images that you want to use, you can upload them to your Reel:

1. Tap the gallery icon in the bottom-left corner of the Reels editor.

2. Select the desired videos or photos from your device.

3. Arrange the clips in your preferred order.

Step 3: Editing Your Reel

Editing is where the magic happens, allowing you to add creativity and polish to your Reel. Facebook provides various tools to enhance your video:

3.1 Adding Music

Music is a powerful way to enhance the mood and tone of your Reel.

1. Tap the music note icon to access Facebook's library of licensed tracks.

2. Browse by genre, mood, or trending songs to find the perfect soundtrack.

3. Select a section of the song to use, adjusting it to fit your Reel's timing.

3.2 Applying Filters and Effects

Filters and effects can make your Reel more visually appealing.

1. Tap the effects icon to browse a wide range of options, including color filters, AR effects, and visual enhancements.

2. Test out different effects in real-time by tapping them while recording or applying them to pre-recorded clips.

3. Experiment with multiple effects to find the one that suits your content.

3.3 Adding Text and Stickers

Text and stickers can add context or personality to your Reel.

1. Tap the "Text" icon to type captions or messages.

2. Customize the font, size, color, and alignment of your text.

3. Use stickers to include emojis, GIFs, or other fun elements. Facebook also offers location and hashtag stickers to make your Reel more discoverable.

3.4 Adjusting Clip Lengths

Fine-tune your Reel by trimming or rearranging clips:

1. Tap a clip in the timeline to select it.

2. Use the trimming handles to adjust the start and end points of the clip.

3. Drag and drop clips to rearrange their order.

3.5 Adding Transitions

Smooth transitions between clips can elevate the professionalism of your Reel.

1. Facebook provides automatic transitions when clips are played sequentially.

2. Experiment with quick cuts or fades to match the rhythm of your Reel.

Step 4: Publishing Your Reel

Once you're satisfied with your Reel, it's time to share it with the world.

4.1 Writing a Caption

Write a short and engaging caption to accompany your Reel.

- Use a compelling hook or question to grab attention.

- Include relevant hashtags to increase discoverability.

4.2 Choosing an Audience

Select who can view your Reel:

1. Public: Anyone on Facebook can see your Reel.

2. Friends: Only your Facebook friends can view it.

3. Custom: Limit visibility to specific friends or groups.

4.3 Adding a Thumbnail

Choose a thumbnail that represents your Reel.

1. Tap the thumbnail icon and select an image from your Reel or upload a custom image.

2. Make sure the thumbnail is clear and visually appealing.

4.4 Posting or Saving as a Draft

If you're ready to share your Reel, tap the "Post" button. Alternatively, you can save it as a draft to make further edits later.

Tips for Creating Engaging Reels

1. **Be Authentic:** Share content that reflects your personality or brand values.

2. **Keep It Short and Sweet:** Aim for concise, impactful storytelling.

3. **Follow Trends:** Participate in trending challenges or use popular songs to increase visibility.

4. **Engage with Your Audience:** Respond to comments and encourage interaction.

Conclusion

Creating and editing Reels on Facebook is a fantastic way to share your creativity, connect with others, and even grow your online presence. By mastering the tools and techniques outlined in this section, you can create visually stunning and highly engaging Reels that resonate with your audience. Remember, practice makes perfect, so don't hesitate to experiment and explore the full potential of this powerful feature.

4.3 Managing Your Content

4.3.1 Editing or Deleting Posts

Managing your content on Facebook is essential for maintaining a polished online presence, ensuring your posts align with your personal or professional goals, and avoiding misunderstandings. Facebook provides intuitive tools to edit or delete posts, whether to correct a mistake, update information, or remove content that no longer reflects your views. This section will guide you step-by-step through the processes, offering detailed instructions and practical tips.

Why Edit or Delete Posts?

Before diving into the steps, it's important to understand why managing your content is critical:

- **Correcting Errors**: Spelling mistakes, incorrect dates, or broken links in a post can leave a poor impression.

- **Updating Information**: You may need to revise a post with new details, such as event updates or project progress.

- **Removing Inappropriate Content**: As your views or circumstances change, certain posts might no longer represent your image or values.

- **Improving Engagement**: A post with an unclear message or low interaction can benefit from edits to make it more appealing.

How to Edit a Facebook Post

Editing a post allows you to refine the content without losing its existing likes, comments, or shares. Here's how you can do it:

Step 1: Locate the Post You Want to Edit

1. Log into your Facebook account and navigate to your **Profile** or the **Page** where the post is located.

2. Scroll down your timeline or use the **Activity Log** to quickly find older posts. The Activity Log is accessible via:

   o Desktop: Click on your profile photo > Select **Activity Log** from the menu.

   o Mobile: Tap on your profile picture > Tap the three dots (•••) > Select **Activity Log**.

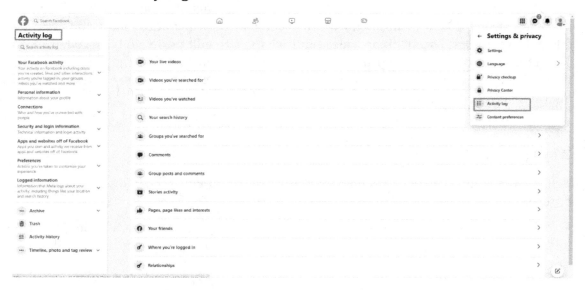

Step 2: Access the Edit Option

1. Once you've located the post, click the three dots (•••) in the top-right corner of the post.

2. From the dropdown menu, select **Edit Post**.

Step 3: Make Your Changes

1. Edit the text, replace photos or videos, or update links as needed.

2. You can also adjust the audience settings by clicking the small globe or lock icon, allowing you to control who can view the updated post.

3. If applicable, tag additional friends, pages, or locations to improve visibility.

Step 4: Save Your Changes

1. After making the necessary edits, click **Save** to update the post.

2. Facebook will display a small note indicating that the post has been edited. Viewers can click on this note to see the edit history of the post.

Tips for Editing Posts

- **Avoid Over-Editing**: Constantly changing a post can confuse your audience. Ensure the content is final before posting.

- **Be Transparent**: If you edit critical information, such as event times or important details, consider adding a note in the comments to notify your audience.

- **Check Links**: Always test any links you've included to ensure they work correctly after editing.

How to Delete a Facebook Post

Deleting a post is a straightforward way to remove content that is outdated, irrelevant, or inappropriate. Keep in mind that deleted posts cannot be recovered, so it's best to double-check before taking action.

Step 1: Locate the Post You Want to Delete

1. Follow the same steps as outlined above to locate the post in your timeline or Activity Log.

Step 2: Access the Delete Option

1. Click the three dots (•••) in the top-right corner of the post.

2. From the dropdown menu, select **Move to Trash** (formerly "Delete Post").

Step 3: Confirm the Deletion

1. Facebook will prompt you to confirm the action. Click **Move to Trash** to proceed.

2. Deleted posts are stored in the **Trash** for 30 days, during which you can restore them if needed. After 30 days, the post will be permanently deleted.

How to Restore or Permanently Delete Posts from Trash

1. Go to your profile and click the three dots (•••) > Select **Activity Log**.

2. Under Activity Log, find the **Trash** section.

3. Locate the post you want to restore or permanently delete.

4. Click **Restore** to bring the post back to your timeline, or click **Delete** to remove it permanently.

Tips for Deleting Posts

- **Archive Instead of Deleting**: If you want to temporarily hide a post instead of deleting it, use the **Archive** option. Archived posts are only visible to you and can be restored at any time.

- **Batch Deletion**: Use the Manage Posts feature to delete multiple posts at once. This is especially useful when cleaning up old content.

When to Edit vs. Delete

Knowing whether to edit or delete a post depends on the context:

- **Edit**: Use this option to correct minor mistakes, such as typos or outdated links, while keeping the original engagement (likes, comments) intact.

- **Delete**: This is the best choice for posts that are irrelevant, inappropriate, or no longer align with your goals.

Practical Scenarios for Managing Posts

Scenario 1: Correcting a Typo in a Popular Post

Imagine you've posted about a milestone event, but there's a spelling error. Editing the post allows you to fix the typo without losing the likes and comments it has already received.

Scenario 2: Updating Event Information

If you shared a post about an upcoming event and the time or location changes, you can edit the post to reflect the new details. Additionally, comment on the post to highlight the update.

Scenario 3: Deleting an Irrelevant Post

You shared a promotional post about a limited-time offer that has expired. Deleting the post ensures your timeline remains up-to-date and relevant to your audience.

Best Practices for Managing Your Content

1. **Regular Content Reviews**: Periodically review your old posts to ensure they still align with your personal or professional brand.

2. **Use Scheduled Posts**: For future content, use Facebook's scheduling feature to carefully plan and review posts before they go live.

3. **Monitor Post Performance**: Use Facebook Insights to evaluate which posts resonate with your audience and adjust your strategy accordingly.

4. **Respond to Feedback**: If someone points out an error in your post, address it promptly by editing the content or acknowledging the feedback in the comments.

5. **Keep an Eye on Privacy**: Regularly check who can see your posts by reviewing your privacy settings. Adjust as needed to maintain control over your content.

By mastering the tools to edit and delete posts on Facebook, you can ensure your content remains polished, accurate, and aligned with your goals. Whether you're maintaining a personal profile or managing a business page, these skills are essential for presenting your best self online.

4.3.2 Controlling Who Can See Your Posts

Sharing content on Facebook is one of the platform's core functionalities, but understanding who can see your posts is equally important. Facebook offers a wide array of privacy settings to ensure that you share your content only with the audience you choose. Whether you're posting personal updates, photos, or professional content, knowing how to control visibility helps you safeguard your privacy, manage your online presence, and connect effectively with the right people.

This section will guide you through the tools and settings available to control who can see your posts on Facebook, from managing individual posts to configuring default privacy settings.

Understanding Facebook's Privacy Options

Facebook provides several audience options when you create or manage a post. Here's an overview of the most common choices:

1. **Public**: Your post will be visible to anyone on Facebook or even people without an account. This option is suitable for content you want to share broadly, such as public announcements or professional updates.

2. **Friends**: Only people on your friends list can see your post. This is ideal for personal updates meant for a more private audience.

3. **Friends Except**: Share your post with all your friends except specific individuals you select. This is useful if you want to exclude certain people from seeing a particular update.

4. **Specific Friends**: Share your post with a select group of friends. This is perfect for private content meant for a smaller, specific audience.

5. **Only Me**: Your post is visible only to you. This option is often used for personal notes or drafts.

6. **Custom**: Customize the audience by including or excluding specific friends, groups, or lists.

Setting the Privacy for a New Post

When you create a new post, Facebook allows you to choose its audience directly:

1. **Step 1: Open the Post Editor**

   o Start by clicking on the "What's on your mind?" box at the top of your News Feed or profile.

2. **Step 2: Click the Privacy Dropdown Menu**

   o Below your name, you'll see a small dropdown menu (defaulted to "Friends," "Public," or another setting based on your preferences). Click it to open the audience selector.

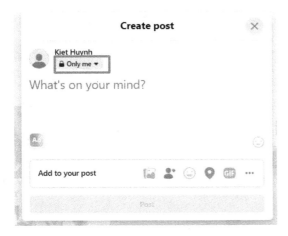

3. **Step 3: Select Your Audience**

   o Choose one of the available options: Public, Friends, Friends Except, Specific Friends, or Only Me.

   o If you choose "Custom," you can manually include or exclude people or groups.

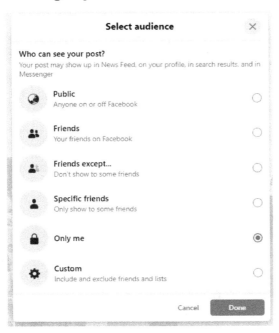

4. **Step 4: Post Your Content**

    o   Once you've selected your audience, proceed to write and share your post.

Managing Privacy for Existing Posts

Sometimes, you may want to adjust the visibility of a post you've already shared. Here's how:

1. **Locate the Post**

    o   Navigate to your profile or the specific location where the post is visible.

2. **Click the Privacy Icon**

    o   Each post has a small icon next to the timestamp (e.g., a globe for Public, two silhouettes for Friends). Click this icon to open the audience selector.

3. **Choose a New Audience**

    o   Select a new audience from the dropdown menu. The change will apply immediately.

4. **Check Audience Overlap**

    o   If you've customized the audience, you can double-check who is included or excluded by clicking "See More" in the privacy options.

Setting a Default Privacy for Future Posts

If you don't want to manually select the audience for each post, Facebook allows you to set a default privacy setting:

1. **Go to Settings**

    o   Click on your profile picture in the top-right corner and select **Settings & Privacy > Settings**.

2. **Navigate to Privacy Settings**

    o   In the left-hand menu, click **Privacy** and locate the section called **Your Activity**.

3. **Set Your Default Audience**

o   Under **Who can see your future posts?**, click **Edit** and choose your preferred default audience.

4.   **Review Your Decision**

o   Facebook will use this setting for all new posts unless you manually change the audience when creating a post.

Using Facebook Lists to Control Your Audience

Lists are a powerful tool for managing your audience. Facebook automatically creates smart lists (e.g., Close Friends, Family, Acquaintances), but you can also create custom lists for specific purposes.

1.   **Create a Custom List**

o   Go to the **Friends** tab on your profile.

o   Click **Custom Lists** and then **Create List**. Name the list and add friends to it.

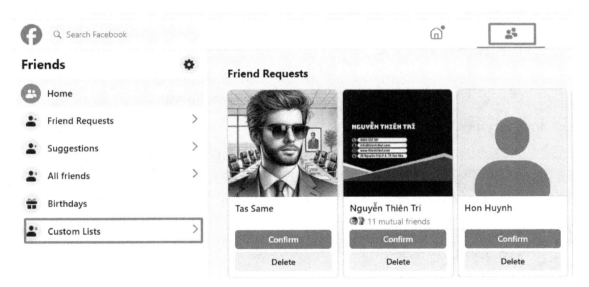

2.   **Use Lists in Privacy Settings**

o   When posting or editing a post, select **Custom** in the audience selector, and include or exclude lists as needed.

3. **Update Lists Regularly**

    o   People's relationships and roles in your life may change over time. Regularly review and update your lists to ensure they reflect your current preferences.

Audience Restrictions for Special Content Types

Certain types of posts may have additional privacy considerations:

1. **Tagged Posts**

    o   When you tag someone in a post, their friends may also see the content. To control this:

        ▪   Go to **Settings & Privacy > Settings > Profile and Tagging**.

        ▪   Under **Who can see posts you're tagged in?**, choose your preferred audience.

        ▪   Enable the **Review tags before they appear** option to approve or deny tags.

2. **Events and Check-Ins**

    o   Posts related to events or check-ins often default to Public. Adjust the privacy manually to avoid oversharing your location.

3. **Shared Posts**

    o   If others share your posts, the audience they share with depends on their privacy settings. Keep this in mind for sensitive content.

Advanced Privacy Tools

1. **Activity Log**

    o   The Activity Log lets you review and manage your posts and their audiences. Access it by navigating to **Settings & Privacy > Activity Log**.

    o   Filter posts by type (e.g., photos, videos, status updates) and adjust the privacy as needed.

2. **Privacy Checkup**

   o Use Facebook's built-in Privacy Checkup tool to review and adjust your settings. This tool walks you through key areas, including post visibility.

3. **Restricting Certain Audiences**

   o If you want to avoid specific individuals seeing your content without unfriending them, use the **Restricted List**:

      ▪ Go to their profile, click **Friends > Edit Friend List**, and select **Restricted**.

Best Practices for Controlling Post Visibility

1. **Think Before You Post**

   o Always consider whether the content is appropriate for the selected audience.

2. **Test Privacy Settings**

   o Use the **View As** tool on your profile to see how your posts appear to others.

      ▪ Go to your profile, click the three dots near the cover photo, and select **View As**.

3. **Review Posts Regularly**

   o Periodically go through your old posts using the Activity Log to ensure their audiences align with your current preferences.

4. **Educate Yourself on Privacy Updates**

   o Facebook frequently updates its privacy tools. Stay informed about changes to maximize your control.

Common Issues and How to Fix Them

1. **Problem: An Audience Setting Isn't Sticking**

o   **Solution**: Clear your browser cache or update the Facebook app. Ensure you've saved the setting correctly before exiting.

2. **Problem: A Post Reaches Unintended Audiences**

    o   **Solution**: Immediately change the audience for the post and review your tagging settings.

3. **Problem: Privacy Settings Are Overridden by Tags**

    o   **Solution**: Turn on **Tag Review** to approve any tags before they appear publicly.

By mastering Facebook's privacy controls, you can confidently share content while protecting your personal and professional boundaries. Always remember: controlling your audience isn't just about privacy—it's about ensuring your content resonates with the right people at the right time.

CHAPTER IV
Mastering Facebook Features

5.1 Messaging with Facebook Messenger

5.1.1 Starting Conversations

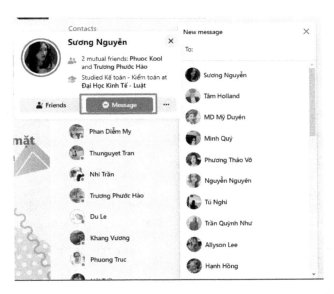

Facebook Messenger is one of the most powerful tools for communication, offering a seamless way to connect with friends, family, colleagues, and even businesses. In this section, we'll guide you step by step on how to start conversations, explore various message types, and optimize your Messenger experience.

Understanding Facebook Messenger

Before diving into starting conversations, it's important to understand the platform itself. Facebook Messenger is a standalone app that integrates with your Facebook account. You can use it to send text messages, photos, videos, voice notes, and even make video and audio calls. Messenger also allows you to create group chats, send emojis, and use stickers to make conversations more engaging.

Step 1: Accessing Facebook Messenger

To begin using Messenger, follow these steps:

1. **On Mobile Devices:**

    o Download the **Facebook Messenger** app from your device's app store (Google Play Store for Android or App Store for iOS).

    o Log in using your Facebook credentials.

    o Grant the app permissions for notifications, contacts, and microphone (if prompted).

2. **On Desktop:**

    o Open your web browser and go to messenger.com.

    o Log in using your Facebook username and password.

3. **Within the Facebook App or Website:**

    o Open the Facebook app or go to the Facebook website.

    o Click on the Messenger icon (usually represented by a speech bubble with a lightning bolt).

Step 2: Starting a New Conversation

To initiate a new conversation, you can either search for a specific person or select them from your friends list. Let's explore these methods in detail:

2.1 Using the Search Bar

- Open Messenger.

- Locate the **Search Bar** at the top of the screen.

- Type the name of the person you want to message.

- Click on their name or profile picture to open the chat window.

- Start typing your message in the text box at the bottom and hit **Send** (usually represented by a paper airplane icon).

2.2 Browsing Your Friends List

- Scroll through your friends list or recent chats to find the person you want to message.

- Tap their profile to open the chat window.

2.3 Messaging Non-Friends

If the person you want to message is not on your friends list:

- Search for their name in the search bar.

- Click on their profile.

- You may see the option to send a message, or they may need to approve your message request first.

Step 3: Crafting Your Message

A conversation begins with a message, and crafting it thoughtfully can make all the difference. Here are some tips for creating engaging and meaningful messages:

3.1 Start with a Greeting

Begin with a friendly greeting like:

- "Hi, how are you?"

- "Hello! I hope you're doing well."

- "Good morning! How's your day going so far?"

3.2 Personalize Your Message

If you're reconnecting with someone after a while, reference a shared memory or mutual interest:

- "It's been ages since we last talked! I still remember our trip to the beach."

- "I saw your recent post about [topic]—that's so interesting!"

3.3 Keep It Clear and Direct

If you're messaging for a specific purpose, state it upfront:

- "I wanted to ask about [specific topic]. Do you have a moment to chat?"

- "Can you help me with [problem/question]?"

3.4 Use Emojis and Stickers Wisely

Adding emojis and stickers can make your message more expressive, but don't overdo it. For example:

- "Hi ☺! How's everything going?"

- "Let's catch up soon! ☐🎉"

Step 4: Enhancing Your Message with Multimedia

Messenger allows you to go beyond simple text messages by incorporating multimedia. This makes your conversations more dynamic and engaging.

4.1 Sending Photos and Videos

- Tap the **Camera Icon** or the **Photo Icon** in the chat box.
- Select an existing photo or video from your gallery, or take one on the spot.
- Add a caption if needed and hit **Send**.

4.2 Using Voice Messages

Voice messages are great for conveying tone and emotion:

- Tap and hold the **Microphone Icon** in the chat box.
- Record your message and release the button to send it.

4.3 Sharing Links

To share a link, simply paste it into the chat box. Messenger will automatically generate a preview, making it easier for the recipient to understand the content.

4.4 Sharing Documents

For work or academic purposes, you can share files:

- Tap the **Attachment Icon** and select a file from your device.

Step 5: Managing Active Conversations

Once you've started a conversation, there are several tools available to enhance and manage it:

5.1 Pinning Chats

To keep important conversations at the top of your chat list:

- Long press the conversation and select **Pin Chat**.

5.2 Reacting to Messages

Express your emotions by reacting to specific messages:

- Tap and hold the message to see reaction options (like, love, laugh, sad, etc.).

- Select the reaction that best fits your response.

5.3 Using Quick Replies

Messenger offers suggestions for quick replies based on the conversation context. These can save time when responding.

Common Scenarios and How to Handle Them

1. **Starting Conversations with Strangers:**

   o Be polite and introduce yourself.

   o State your reason for messaging clearly to avoid confusion.

2. **Reaching Out for Professional Purposes:**

   o Use a formal tone.

   o Include context, such as how you found their profile or why you're reaching out.

3. **Reconnecting After a Long Time:**

   o Acknowledge the time gap: "It's been a while since we last talked!"

   o Update them briefly about your life and ask about theirs.

Best Practices for Starting Conversations

- **Be Respectful:** Always maintain a polite and friendly tone.

- **Be Genuine:** Avoid sounding robotic or overly formal unless the context requires it.

- **Be Patient:** If the recipient doesn't respond immediately, give them time.

By following these steps and tips, you'll be able to confidently start conversations on Facebook Messenger, making the most of this versatile communication tool. Whether you're catching up with friends, networking professionally, or chatting casually, Messenger offers endless possibilities to connect.

5.1.2 Using Voice and Video Calls

Facebook Messenger is a versatile communication tool that not only supports text-based messaging but also enables users to make voice and video calls. This feature is especially useful for staying in touch with friends, family, or colleagues, offering a free and efficient alternative to traditional phone calls. In this section, we'll explore how to use the voice and video call features of Facebook Messenger effectively.

Understanding Voice and Video Calls on Messenger

Voice and video calls on Messenger are accessible through the app on both mobile devices and desktops. They rely on an internet connection, which means you can make calls without worrying about phone carrier charges. All you need is a stable Wi-Fi connection or sufficient mobile data.

Here are some key points to note:

- Voice calls are audio-only, similar to a phone call but conducted over the internet.

- Video calls allow participants to see each other in real-time, making it ideal for personal conversations, virtual meetings, or even group discussions.

- Both options are end-to-end encrypted, ensuring that your calls remain private and secure.

Getting Started with Voice Calls on Messenger

1. Initiating a Voice Call

To start a voice call, follow these steps:

1. **Open Messenger:** Launch the Facebook Messenger app on your mobile device or open it in a web browser.

2. **Select a Contact:** Find the person you want to call by either scrolling through your chats or using the search bar at the top of the screen.

3. **Tap the Phone Icon:** Once you open the chat with your selected contact, look for the phone icon in the top-right corner of the screen. Tap it to initiate a voice call.

4. **Wait for Connection:** The recipient will receive a call notification. Once they accept the call, you can start speaking.

2. Features During a Voice Call

While on a voice call, Messenger offers several features to enhance your experience:

- **Mute Button:** If you need to mute yourself during the call, tap the microphone icon. Tap it again to unmute.

- **Speakerphone:** Switch to speaker mode by tapping the speaker icon. This is useful if you want to talk hands-free.

- **End Call:** To end the call, tap the red phone icon.

3. Troubleshooting Voice Call Issues

If you experience issues with voice calls, here are some tips to resolve them:

- **Check Your Internet Connection:** Ensure you have a stable Wi-Fi or mobile data connection.

- **Update the App:** Make sure you're using the latest version of Messenger.

- **Grant Permissions:** Check that Messenger has access to your microphone in your device's settings.

Getting Started with Video Calls on Messenger

1. Initiating a Video Call

Starting a video call is similar to initiating a voice call, with one additional step:

1. **Open Messenger:** Launch the app or web version of Messenger.

2. **Select a Contact:** Open the chat of the person you want to call.

3. **Tap the Camera Icon:** In the top-right corner of the screen, tap the camera icon to start a video call.

4. **Wait for Connection:** The recipient will receive a notification. Once they accept, the video call begins.

2. Features During a Video Call

Messenger video calls include several useful features to enhance your experience:

-   **Switch Cameras:** Toggle between the front and rear cameras by tapping the camera flip icon. This is especially useful if you want to show something around you.

-   **Mute Microphone:** If you don't want to speak, tap the microphone icon to mute yourself.

-   **Turn Off Video:** If you want to switch to a voice-only mode during the call, tap the video icon to turn off your camera.

-   **Share Screen:** On some devices, you can share your screen during the call, which is great for showing documents, photos, or presentations.

-   **Reactions:** Messenger allows you to use emojis like a thumbs-up or heart during video calls to express yourself without interrupting the conversation.

3. Adding More People to a Video Call

Facebook Messenger supports group video calls, allowing you to connect with multiple people at once. To add participants:

-   During an ongoing video call, tap the "Add Person" button (usually represented by a + icon).

- Select the contacts you want to include. They will receive a notification to join the call.

4. Troubleshooting Video Call Issues

If your video call isn't working smoothly, try these solutions:

- **Improve Lighting:** Ensure you're in a well-lit area for better video quality.

- **Check Camera Permissions:** Make sure Messenger has access to your camera in your device's settings.

- **Stabilize Your Internet Connection:** Use a strong Wi-Fi connection or switch to a location with better reception.

- **Restart the App:** Close and reopen Messenger if the video call freezes or doesn't start.

Using Voice and Video Calls on Desktop

Messenger's voice and video call features are also available on desktops through the Messenger website or Facebook.

1. Starting a Call on Desktop

- Open Messenger in your web browser or on the Facebook website.

- Navigate to the chat of the person you want to call.

- Click the phone or camera icon in the chat window to initiate a voice or video call.

2. Features During Desktop Calls

- Use your computer's microphone and camera for seamless communication.

- Share your screen by clicking the screen share button, useful for business meetings or collaborative discussions.

Best Practices for Voice and Video Calls

1. **Ensure Privacy:** Always check your surroundings before starting a video call, especially in public places.

2. **Use Headphones:** For better sound quality and privacy, use headphones or earbuds.

3. **Respect Time Zones:** If you're calling someone in a different country, be mindful of their time zone.

4. **Prepare for Group Calls:** If hosting a group video call, inform participants in advance to ensure availability.

5. **Test Your Equipment:** Before important calls, test your microphone, camera, and internet connection.

Creative Uses for Messenger Calls

1. **Virtual Celebrations:** Host birthday parties or reunions via group video calls.

2. **Remote Work Meetings:** Use screen sharing to collaborate on projects with colleagues.

3. **Online Tutoring:** Teach or learn remotely by using video calls to connect with students or instructors.

4. **Check-Ins with Loved Ones:** Stay connected with family and friends, even if they are far away.

Conclusion

Voice and video calls on Facebook Messenger offer an efficient, cost-effective way to stay connected with people around the world. By mastering the features outlined in this section, you can elevate your communication experience, whether for personal or professional purposes.

5.1.3 Managing Chat Settings

Facebook Messenger offers a variety of settings to customize your chat experience, ensuring it aligns with your preferences and needs. From adjusting privacy settings to organizing your chats and controlling notifications, this section will guide you through the essential features available for managing your Messenger settings effectively.

Understanding the Messenger Settings Menu

Before diving into specific settings, it's important to know where to find the Messenger settings menu. You can access it by opening the Messenger app on your mobile device or navigating to Messenger via the Facebook website.

- **On Mobile:** Tap your profile picture in the top-left corner of the Messenger home screen to access settings.

- **On Desktop:** Click the gear icon in the bottom-left corner of the Messenger window.

This menu is your hub for managing chat preferences, privacy controls, and customization options.

1. Customizing Chat Notifications

Notifications play a critical role in keeping you informed about messages, but they can become overwhelming if not managed properly. Here's how to take control:

a. Turning Notifications On or Off

1. Open the settings menu.

2. Look for the "Notifications & Sounds" option.

3. Toggle the switch to turn all notifications on or off.

b. Customizing Notifications for Specific Chats: If you prefer to silence notifications for specific conversations:

1. Open the chat you want to mute.

2. Tap the name of the person or group at the top of the screen.

3. Select **"Mute Notifications"** and choose a duration (e.g., 15 minutes, 1 hour, or indefinitely).

c. Adjusting Sound and Vibration Settings: You can modify how notifications sound and feel:

1. In the "Notifications & Sounds" menu, select **"Ringtone"** or **"Notification Sound."**

2. Choose a sound from the available options or upload your own custom tone.

3. Adjust vibration intensity or disable it entirely if preferred.

2. Managing Active Status

Your active status lets your friends know when you're online and available to chat. However, there might be times when you prefer to appear offline.

a. Hiding Your Active Status

1. Go to your settings menu.

2. Select **"Active Status."**

3. Toggle the switch to turn it off.

b. Managing Exceptions: You can customize your active status visibility by creating exceptions:

1. Under **"Active Status,"** tap **"Add Exceptions."**

2. Choose specific people who can see or not see your active status.

3. Organizing and Archiving Chats

Keeping your Messenger inbox organized can save time and make conversations easier to navigate.

a. Archiving Old Chats: Archiving removes chats from your main inbox without deleting them:

1. Swipe left on a chat (mobile) or hover over it and click the three dots (desktop).

2. Select **"Archive."**

3. Archived chats can be found by searching the person's name in the search bar.

b. Pinning Important Conversations: Pinning ensures your most-used chats stay at the top of your inbox:

1. Open the chat you want to pin.

2. Tap the name of the person or group and select **"Pin Conversation."**

c. Using Message Filters: On desktop, you can filter your inbox into categories such as unread, archived, or message requests by clicking **"Filters"** in the left-hand menu.

4. Privacy Settings in Messenger

Messenger allows you to control who can contact you and how they can interact with you.

a. Message Requests: Not all messages go straight to your inbox. Message requests filter messages from people you're not friends with.

1. Open the settings menu and select **"Privacy."**

2. Tap **"Message Delivery."**

3. Set preferences for who can send you messages directly (e.g., friends, friends of friends, or others).

b. Blocking Users: If you no longer want to communicate with someone:

1. Open the chat with that person.

2. Tap their name at the top of the screen.

3. Scroll down and select **"Block."** You can block just their messages or block them entirely on Facebook.

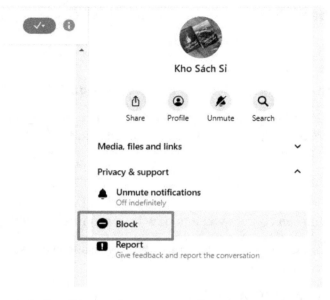

c. Restricting Users: Restricting allows you to limit interactions without fully blocking someone:

1. Open a chat, tap the person's name, and select **"Restrict."**

2. Restricted users can't see your active status or know if you've read their messages.

5. Customizing Chat Appearance

Messenger offers several ways to personalize your chat experience:

a. Changing Chat Colors and Themes

1. Open the chat you want to customize.

2. Tap the person's name at the top.

3. Select **"Theme"** and choose from the available options.

b. Assigning Nicknames: You can add nicknames for your contacts to make chats more personalized:

1. Open a chat, tap the person's name, and select **"Nicknames."**

2. Enter a nickname and save it.

c. Using Chat Emojis: Set a default emoji for each chat:

1. Tap the person's name and select **"Emoji."**

2. Choose your preferred emoji from the list.

6. Managing Data and Storage Usage

Messenger allows you to monitor and control how much data and storage it uses on your device.

a. Checking Data Usage

1. Go to the settings menu.

2. Tap **"Data Saver."**

3. Turn on **"Data Saver"** to reduce data consumption, especially when using mobile networks.

b. Clearing Chat History and Media Files

1. Open the settings menu and select **"Storage."**

2. View how much storage each conversation is using.

3. Delete unnecessary files or clear the conversation history to free up space.

7. Handling Group Chats

Group chats are a popular Messenger feature, and managing them effectively is key to ensuring a smooth experience.

a. Customizing Group Settings

1. Open the group chat and tap the group name at the top.

2. Modify settings such as notifications, nicknames, and theme.

b. Adding or Removing Members

1. Open the group settings.

2. Tap **"Add People"** or **"Remove from Group."**

c. Leaving or Deleting Groups

1. To leave a group, tap **"Leave Group"** in the group settings.

2. If you're the group creator, you can delete the group by removing all members first and then leaving the group.

---

8. Ensuring Accessibility in Messenger

Facebook Messenger includes features for users with accessibility needs:

a. Using Voice Commands

1. Enable voice typing to send messages hands-free.

2. Use built-in screen readers to navigate Messenger.

b. Enlarging Text Size

1. Adjust text size in your device's accessibility settings.

2. Messenger will follow the system-wide settings for larger text.

By mastering these settings and features, you can take full control of your Messenger experience, ensuring it's tailored to your preferences and meets your needs. From privacy and notifications to personalization and accessibility, these tools make Facebook Messenger a versatile and user-friendly platform for communication.

5.2 Events and Invitations

5.2.1 Creating an Event

Facebook Events are a powerful tool that allows users to create and manage gatherings, whether they are personal, professional, or community-based. Whether you're organizing a birthday party, a business seminar, a charity fundraiser, or a casual get-together, Facebook Events make it easy to invite people, share details, and keep everyone informed. In this section, we will provide a step-by-step guide to creating an event on Facebook, covering all the essential features, tips, and best practices to ensure your event is a success.

Step 1: Navigate to the Events Section

To start creating an event, follow these steps:

1. **Access the Events Tab**:

    o On the desktop, click the **"Events"** tab located in the left-hand menu of your Facebook homepage.

    o On mobile, tap the **Menu** button (three horizontal lines) and scroll down to find the **Events** option.

2. **Click or Tap "Create Event"**: Once you're in the Events section, look for the **"Create New Event"** button.

Step 2: Choose the Event Type

Facebook allows you to choose between two types of events:

1. **Private Event**:

   o Ideal for personal gatherings like birthday parties, family reunions, or small group meetings.

   o Only invited guests can see the event details and RSVP.

   o Guests cannot share the event with others.

2. **Public Event**:

   o Perfect for events open to the public, such as workshops, concerts, or community fundraisers.

   o Visible to anyone on Facebook, and attendees can share the event with their network.

   o Public events allow you to gain wider reach and attract more participants.

Choose the event type based on the nature and audience of your gathering.

Step 3: Fill in Event Details

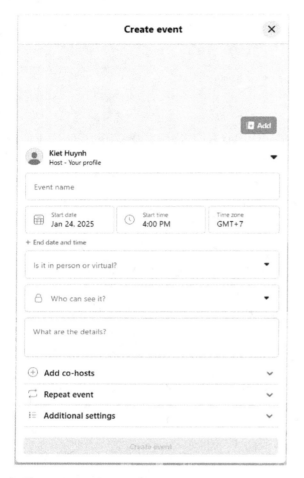

After selecting the event type, you'll need to fill out the key details to make your event informative and engaging.

1. **Event Name**:

   o   Choose a clear and compelling name for your event.

   o   Keep it short and specific (e.g., "John's 30th Birthday Bash" or "Digital Marketing Workshop 2025").

2. **Date and Time**:

   o   Select the start and end date and time for your event.

   o   Consider including a buffer time for attendees to arrive early if needed.

3. **Location**:

    o   Enter a physical address for in-person events or select **Online Event** for virtual gatherings.

    o   For online events, you can include details like a Zoom link or a live-streaming platform.

4. **Description**:

    o   Write a detailed and engaging description of your event. Include important details like:

        ▪   What the event is about.

        ▪   Who the event is for.

        ▪   Any special instructions (e.g., dress code, items to bring).

    o   Use bullet points to make it easy to read.

5. **Cover Photo or Video**:

    o   Upload an eye-catching image or video that represents your event.

    o   Ensure the dimensions are optimized for Facebook (1920x1005 pixels).

    o   A well-designed cover photo can significantly increase interest and attendance.

Step 4: Add Additional Options

Facebook provides additional settings to customize your event further:

1. **Event Settings**:

    o   Enable or disable the ability for attendees to invite others (for private events).

    o   Choose whether you want guests to see the guest list.

2. **Schedule Posts**:

    o   Use the event page to post updates, reminders, or announcements leading up to the event.

       ○   Schedule posts to automatically go live at specific times.

3. **Co-Hosts**:

       ○   Add co-hosts to help you manage the event. Co-hosts can edit event details, invite attendees, and post updates.

Step 5: Publish and Share the Event

1. **Preview the Event**:

       ○   Before publishing, review all the details to ensure accuracy.

       ○   Check for typos or missing information.

2. **Click "Publish"**:

       ○   Once you're satisfied, click the **"Publish"** button to make the event live.

3. **Share the Event**:

       ○   Share the event on your timeline, in relevant groups, or on your business page.

       ○   For public events, encourage attendees to share the event with their networks.

Step 6: Engage with Attendees

After your event is live, maintaining engagement with attendees is crucial:

1. **Respond to Questions**:

       ○   Monitor the event page for questions or comments and respond promptly.

       ○   This helps build excitement and ensures attendees have all the necessary information.

2. **Post Updates**:

       ○   Share reminders as the event date approaches.

       ○   Post teasers, such as sneak peeks of activities, guest speakers, or prizes.

3. **Interact with Guests**:

    o Like or reply to posts and RSVPs to show appreciation for attendees' interest.

Tips for Creating a Successful Event

1. **Promote Early**:

    o Create the event at least a few weeks in advance to give people enough time to plan.

2. **Encourage RSVPs**:

    o Ask people to RSVP to help you estimate attendance numbers.

3. **Use Targeted Invites**:

    o For private events, invite specific friends or groups who are most likely to attend.

4. **Cross-Promote**:

    o Promote the event on other social media platforms or through email newsletters.

5. **Create Buzz**:

    o Use engaging visuals, hashtags, or countdown posts to generate excitement.

6. **Follow Up After the Event**:

    o Post thank-you messages or event highlights to maintain engagement and encourage feedback.

By following these steps and tips, you can create a Facebook Event that is not only informative but also engaging and memorable. Whether it's a small private gathering or a large-scale public event, Facebook's event tools provide everything you need to ensure success.

5.2.2 RSVP to Events

Facebook Events is a powerful tool that allows users to organize gatherings, celebrations, or even professional meetings. Whether it's a birthday party, a virtual webinar, or a community fundraiser, events on Facebook make it easy to invite others and keep track of attendance. RSVP, which stands for "Répondez S'il Vous Plaît" (a French term meaning "please respond"), is an integral part of the Facebook Events feature, allowing attendees to confirm their participation. In this section, we'll guide you through the steps of RSVPing to events on Facebook and provide insights into making the most of this feature.

Understanding RSVP Options

When you are invited to a Facebook event, you'll notice three main RSVP options:

- **Going**: Indicates that you plan to attend the event.

- **Maybe/Interested**: Shows that you are considering attending but haven't decided yet.

- **Not Going**: Lets the organizer know you won't be attending.

Each RSVP option is designed to help both you and the event organizer understand the level of participation. Selecting the right response is important, as it not only informs the host but also provides you with tailored updates about the event.

How to RSVP to an Event on Facebook

RSVPing to a Facebook event is a straightforward process, but it varies slightly depending on the device you're using. Follow these detailed steps to ensure your RSVP is properly submitted:

1. On the Facebook App (Mobile)

1. **Open Facebook**: Launch the Facebook app on your smartphone or tablet.

2. **Navigate to Events**: Tap the three horizontal lines (menu) in the bottom-right corner (iOS) or top-right corner (Android). Select **Events** from the menu.

3. **Find the Event**:

- o   If you've been invited, look under the **Invites** tab.

- o   To search for public events, use the search bar at the top of the Events page.

4. **View the Event Details**: Tap on the event to open its page and review key details such as date, time, location, and description.

5. **RSVP**: Below the event name, you'll see the RSVP options: **Going, Maybe/Interested**, or **Not Going**. Select the option that reflects your intent.

- o   If you choose **Going** or **Interested**, the event will be added to your calendar on Facebook for easy tracking.

2. On the Desktop (Web Browser)

1. **Log In to Facebook**: Go to facebook.com and log in with your credentials.

2. **Access Events**:

- o   On the left-hand menu, click on **Events**.

- o   If invited, look for the event under the **Invitations** section.

3. **Open the Event Page**: Click on the event name to view all its details.

4. **RSVP**: At the top of the event page, you'll see the RSVP buttons: **Going, Maybe/Interested**, or **Not Going**. Select your preferred response.

Modifying Your RSVP

Life can be unpredictable, and plans might change. Facebook makes it easy to update your RSVP if needed:

- Open the event page on your mobile app or desktop.

- Tap or click your current RSVP status (e.g., **Going**) to reveal the options again.

- Choose a new option (**Maybe/Interested** or **Not Going**) as necessary.

This flexibility ensures that both you and the event organizer are kept up-to-date with your plans.

Why RSVP Matters

RSVPing serves several important purposes for both attendees and organizers:

1. **Event Planning**: It helps organizers estimate the number of attendees, which is critical for arranging food, seating, or other logistics.

2. **Communication**: Once you RSVP, you'll receive notifications about event updates, such as changes in time or location.

3. **Calendar Integration**: When you RSVP as **Going** or **Interested**, the event is automatically added to your Facebook calendar.

How to Engage with an Event After RSVP

RSVPing is just the beginning of your interaction with a Facebook event. Here's how you can make the most of the experience:

1. Share the Event

If you're attending an event you're excited about, consider sharing it with your friends.

- On the event page, tap or click **Share**.

- Choose whether to share it on your timeline, in a group, or directly with friends via Messenger.

2. Ask Questions

Use the event's discussion section to ask questions or share your thoughts. For example, you might inquire about parking, dress code, or specific event details.

3. Invite Others

Some events allow attendees to invite their friends. If you think someone in your network would enjoy the event, click **Invite** on the event page and select their name.

4. Engage During the Event

- If the event includes live updates, such as a livestream, comment or react in real-time to connect with other attendees.

- Share photos or videos from the event to the discussion section, fostering a sense of community.

Tips for RSVP Etiquette

When RSVPing to Facebook events, keep the following tips in mind:

1. **Be Prompt**: Respond to invitations as soon as possible to help the organizer plan effectively.

2. **Keep the Organizer Updated**: If your plans change, update your RSVP promptly.

3. **Respect Private Events**: If the event is private, avoid sharing details publicly unless the organizer has given permission.

4. **Follow Through**: If you RSVP as **Going**, make every effort to attend or notify the host if you can't make it.

Using RSVP for Virtual Events

With the rise of virtual events, Facebook's RSVP feature has become even more useful. When attending an online event:

- Make sure you have the correct link or access code, often provided in the event description.

- Set reminders so you don't forget to join the event at the scheduled time.

- Test your internet connection and devices beforehand to ensure smooth participation.

Common Problems and How to Solve Them

1. **Missing Event Invitations**: If you don't see an invitation, check your notifications or the **Invites** section under Events.

2. **Accidental RSVP**: Simply revisit the event page and update your response.

3. **Event Cancellations**: If an event is canceled, the organizer will usually update the page and notify attendees.

By mastering the RSVP feature on Facebook, you can stay organized, engage meaningfully with others, and make the most of your social interactions. Whether you're attending a birthday party, a concert, or a professional webinar, your RSVP is a simple yet powerful way to stay connected.

5.2.3 Managing Invitations

Managing invitations on Facebook is an essential skill for organizing events, maintaining connections, and ensuring smooth communication with your invitees. Whether you're hosting a casual get-together, a professional event, or a community activity, understanding how to effectively manage invitations can make all the difference in event attendance and engagement. In this section, we'll explore step-by-step processes, tools, and best practices for handling Facebook invitations like a pro.

1. Understanding Facebook Invitations

When you create an event on Facebook, invitations serve as the primary way to inform and engage potential attendees. These invitations notify users about the event and provide them with options to respond (e.g., "Going," "Maybe," or "Not Going"). Managing these responses efficiently ensures you can prepare appropriately and keep attendees informed.

2. Viewing and Tracking Invitation Responses

To manage invitations, you first need to track who has responded and their chosen attendance status. Follow these steps:

Step 1: Access Your Event Page

1. Open Facebook on your desktop or mobile device.

2. Navigate to the event by either clicking on the **Events** section in the left-hand menu (on desktop) or tapping the three horizontal lines and selecting **Events** on mobile.

3. Click on the specific event you want to manage.

Step 2: View the Guest List

1. On the event page, scroll down to the section labeled **Guests** or **Invited.**

2. You'll see the following categories:

- o **Going:** Guests who have confirmed their attendance.

- o **Maybe:** Guests who are undecided.

- o **Invited:** Guests who have yet to respond.

- o **Not Going:** Guests who declined the invitation.

Step 3: Analyze Responses

- Pay close attention to the "Going" and "Maybe" categories to estimate attendance.

- Use the "Invited" list to identify who hasn't responded yet and consider sending follow-ups.

---

3. Sending Reminder Notifications to Invitees

One of the most valuable features of Facebook events is the ability to remind guests who haven't RSVP'd yet. Here's how to send reminders:

Step 1: Open the Event

1. Navigate to your event page.

2. Click on the **Guests** tab to view the list of invitees.

Step 2: Send Reminder Messages

1. For each person in the "Invited" or "Maybe" list, you'll see an option to send a reminder.

2. Click **Send Reminder** next to their name. Facebook will send a notification prompting them to RSVP.

Pro Tip: Avoid overusing reminders, as excessive notifications can irritate invitees. Limit reminders to one or two strategic times, such as a week before the event and the day before the event.

---

4. Communicating with Invitees

Effective communication is key to ensuring a successful event. Facebook provides several tools to help you stay in touch with your invitees:

4.1 Using the Event Discussion Board

1. Post updates, reminders, and additional details on the event's **Discussion** board.

2. Tag attendees in your posts to ensure they see important updates.

3. Use engaging language to encourage interaction (e.g., "We're so excited to see everyone tomorrow! Don't forget to bring your tickets!").

4.2 Sending Private Messages: For high-priority attendees or VIP guests, consider sending a direct message:

1. Click on the name of an invitee from the guest list.

2. Use Messenger to send a personalized message, such as, "Hi [Name], I hope you can join us for [Event Name]! Let me know if you have any questions."

---

5. Managing Changes and Cancellations

Unexpected changes or cancellations may occur, and it's essential to communicate these promptly:

5.1 Updating Event Details: If the event's date, time, or location changes:

1. Go to the **Edit Event** option on your event page.

2. Update the relevant details.

3. Post an announcement in the event discussion and tag invitees.

5.2 Canceling an Event: If the event must be canceled:

1. Navigate to the event page and click on **Edit Event.**

2. Select **Cancel Event.**

3. Notify invitees using a post, explaining the reason for the cancellation and apologizing for any inconvenience.

---

6. Encouraging Last-Minute RSVPs

Sometimes, people need a little nudge to commit to attending. Encourage last-minute RSVPs using these strategies:

6.1 Posting a Countdown Reminder: Create a post that highlights how close the event is:

- "Only 2 days left until [Event Name]! Don't forget to RSVP!"

6.2 Highlighting Exciting Event Features: Mention special highlights of the event, such as guest speakers, giveaways, or exclusive activities:

- "We're thrilled to announce that [Special Guest] will be joining us! RSVP now to secure your spot!"

6.3 Leveraging Friends of Invitees: If your event is public, attendees can invite their friends. Encourage your confirmed guests to share the event with their network to boost attendance.

---

7. Best Practices for Managing Invitations

Follow these tips to ensure a smooth invitation management process:

7.1 Be Timely and Proactive

- Send invitations at least 2-3 weeks in advance to give people time to plan.

- Follow up with reminders as the event approaches.

7.2 Personalize Invitations When Possible

- People are more likely to respond when they feel personally invited. Include a brief, friendly message when sending invitations.

7.3 Monitor and Respond to Guest Questions

- Check the event page regularly for comments or questions from invitees. Respond promptly to clarify details and build excitement.

7.4 Respect Declines

- Avoid pressuring guests who have indicated they're not going. Focus on engaging those who are still undecided.

---

8. Tools for Post-Event Follow-Up

Managing invitations doesn't stop when the event ends. Post-event follow-up is crucial for maintaining relationships:

8.1 Thanking Attendees: Post a thank-you message on the event page and tag attendees:

- "Thank you all for coming to [Event Name]! We loved having you there and hope to see you at our next event!"

8.2 Gathering Feedback: Create a poll or post asking for feedback to improve future events:

- "What did you enjoy most about [Event Name]? Let us know your thoughts!"

8.3 Sharing Event Highlights: Upload photos, videos, or a summary of the event to keep the excitement alive and encourage others to attend future events.

Conclusion

Managing invitations effectively is the backbone of organizing a successful event on Facebook. By tracking responses, sending timely reminders, and communicating with attendees, you can ensure your event is well-attended and engaging. Implement these steps and strategies to streamline your invitation process and create memorable experiences for your guests.

5.3 Marketplace: Buying and Selling

5.3.1 Browsing Marketplace Listings

The **Facebook Marketplace** has transformed how people buy and sell locally, making it easier than ever to find items that suit your needs without leaving the app. Whether you're hunting for a second-hand bicycle, a piece of vintage furniture, or even real estate, Facebook Marketplace is a one-stop destination for discovering deals in your area. In this section, we'll explore how to navigate and browse Marketplace listings effectively, ensuring you get the most out of this feature.

Understanding Facebook Marketplace

Before diving into browsing, it's important to understand what the Marketplace is and how it works:

- **What is Facebook Marketplace?** Facebook Marketplace is a platform within Facebook where users can buy, sell, and trade goods or services. It functions as an online classified system, connecting local buyers and sellers directly.

- **How Does It Work?** Sellers create listings for items they want to sell, including photos, descriptions, prices, and pickup locations. Buyers can then browse these listings, filter results, and contact sellers through Facebook Messenger.

- **Who Can Use Marketplace?** Anyone with a Facebook account can access the Marketplace, provided it's available in their region. It's free to use, with no additional fees for buying or selling items.

Step-by-Step Guide to Browsing Listings

Let's go through the process of browsing Marketplace listings in detail:

1. Accessing Facebook Marketplace

1. **Log in to Your Facebook Account**: Ensure you're logged in to your account on the Facebook app or website. Marketplace is accessible on both mobile devices and desktops.

2. **Locate the Marketplace Icon**:

   o   On **Mobile**: Tap the "Marketplace" icon (a storefront symbol) located in the bottom or top menu bar, depending on your device.

   o   On **Desktop**: Click the "Marketplace" icon in the left-hand menu.

3. **Explore the Homepage**: Once inside Marketplace, you'll see a homepage featuring recommended items, popular categories, and listings tailored to your location and preferences.

2. Using the Search Bar

The search bar is one of the most powerful tools for browsing Marketplace listings effectively.

1. **Enter Keywords**: Type in specific keywords related to the item you're looking for, such as "laptop," "office desk," or "bicycle."

2. **Refine Your Search**:

   o   Use clear and concise terms. For example, instead of "cheap used phone," search for "iPhone 11 under $500."

   o   Experiment with synonyms or alternative descriptions (e.g., "couch" vs. "sofa").

3. **Search Suggestions**: Facebook might auto-suggest related terms as you type. These suggestions can help you find more accurate results.

3. Filtering Results

Browsing Marketplace becomes easier when you use filters to narrow down your options. Here's how to use them:

1. **Location Filter**:

   o **Set Your Location**: Marketplace defaults to your current location, but you can change it if you're searching in a different area.

   o **Adjust the Radius**: Use the slider to set how far from your location you're willing to search (e.g., within 10 miles or up to 100 miles).

2. **Price Range Filter**:

   o Enter a minimum and maximum price to find items within your budget. For instance, if you're looking for a dining table between $50 and $150, you can specify that range.

3. **Category Filter**:

   o Select a category to focus your search, such as "Electronics," "Home & Garden," "Vehicles," or "Clothing."

4. **Condition Filter**:

   o Choose the condition of the item: **New, Used - Like New, Used - Good**, or **Used - Fair**.

5. **Other Filters**:

   o Depending on the category, you may find additional filters, such as size (for clothing), make and model (for vehicles), or brand (for electronics).

---

4. Browsing Categories

If you're not searching for a specific item, you can explore categories to discover items of interest.

1. **Popular Categories**: Some of the most popular categories include:

   o **Electronics**: Smartphones, laptops, gaming consoles, etc.

   o **Home & Garden**: Furniture, appliances, and décor.

   o **Vehicles**: Cars, motorcycles, bicycles.

     o **Clothing & Accessories**: Men's, women's, and children's fashion.

2. **Subcategories**:

Each main category is divided into subcategories for easier navigation. For instance:

     o Under "Electronics," you might find subcategories like "Laptops," "TVs," or "Cameras."

     o Under "Home & Garden," you might find "Furniture," "Tools," or "Outdoor Equipment."

---

5. Viewing Item Listings

Once you find an item that interests you, click on it to open the listing. Each listing provides detailed information about the item.

đ159

Ho Chi Minh City, Vietnam

1. **Photos**:

   o Check for clear, high-quality photos that show the item from multiple angles.

   o Look for close-ups of important features or possible defects.

2. **Description**:

   o Read the seller's description carefully. It should include details like dimensions, brand, condition, and any flaws.

3. **Price**:

   o Confirm whether the price is fixed or negotiable. Some sellers may include terms like "OBO" (or best offer).

4. **Location**:

   o Check where the item is located and whether the seller offers delivery.

5. **Seller Information**:

o   Look at the seller's profile to gauge trustworthiness. Facebook displays information like how long they've been a Marketplace user and reviews from previous buyers.

6. Saving Listings

If you're not ready to purchase immediately, you can save listings for later.

1. **Click the Save Icon**: Tap the "Save" button on the listing. Saved items are accessible under the "Saved" tab in Marketplace.

2. **Organize Saved Listings**: Use the "Collections" feature to group saved items into categories, such as "Furniture Ideas" or "Electronics Wishlist."

Tips for Effective Browsing

To make your browsing experience more efficient, keep the following tips in mind:

- **Use Specific Filters**: The more specific you are, the easier it is to find what you're looking for.

- **Check Listings Frequently**: New items are added daily, so revisit Marketplace regularly to catch deals before they're gone.

- **Be Cautious of Scams**: If something seems too good to be true, it probably is. Avoid suspicious listings or sellers who refuse to communicate.

Real-Life Example

Imagine you're searching for a dining table:

1. **Search**: Type "dining table" in the search bar.

2. **Filter**: Set the price range between $100 and $300, and limit the search to within 20 miles of your location.

3. **Explore Listings**: Browse the results, check photos, and save any promising options.

4. **Contact Sellers**: Once you find the perfect table, message the seller to confirm availability and discuss pickup.

Conclusion

Browsing Marketplace listings is an intuitive and enjoyable process once you familiarize yourself with the tools and features available. By understanding how to navigate the platform, utilize filters, and evaluate listings, you can confidently find great deals while avoiding potential pitfalls. With Facebook Marketplace, the possibilities are endless—happy browsing!

5.3.2 Creating a Listing

Facebook Marketplace has become a go-to platform for buying and selling items within your local community. Creating a listing on Marketplace is straightforward, but crafting an effective and appealing listing requires attention to detail. This guide will walk you through every step of creating a successful listing, from the technical steps involved to tips for attracting buyers and closing sales.

Step 1: Accessing Facebook Marketplace

Before creating a listing, ensure you know how to access Facebook Marketplace:

1. **On Desktop:**

   o Open your Facebook account and look for the **Marketplace** icon in the main navigation bar (it looks like a storefront). Click on it to access the Marketplace section.

2. **On Mobile App:**

   o Open the Facebook app and tap the **Marketplace** icon at the bottom or top of your screen, depending on your device.

Once you're in the Marketplace, you'll see various options, including "Buy" and "Sell." To create a listing, you'll select the **Sell** option.

Step 2: Choosing the Right Listing Type

When you click on the **Sell** button, you'll need to select the type of listing you want to create. Facebook offers several categories for your item, including:

- **Item for Sale**: For general products like electronics, furniture, clothes, etc.

- **Vehicle for Sale**: For cars, motorcycles, or other vehicles.

- **Property for Sale or Rent**: For real estate listings like homes, apartments, or commercial spaces.

- **Job Openings**: If you're hiring, you can post job opportunities here.

For this example, let's assume you are selling an item. Select **Item for Sale** to proceed.

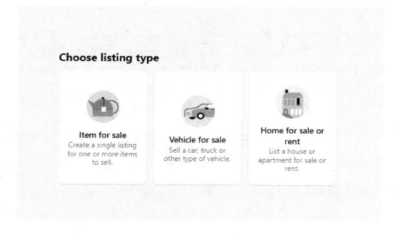

Step 3: Filling Out Listing Details

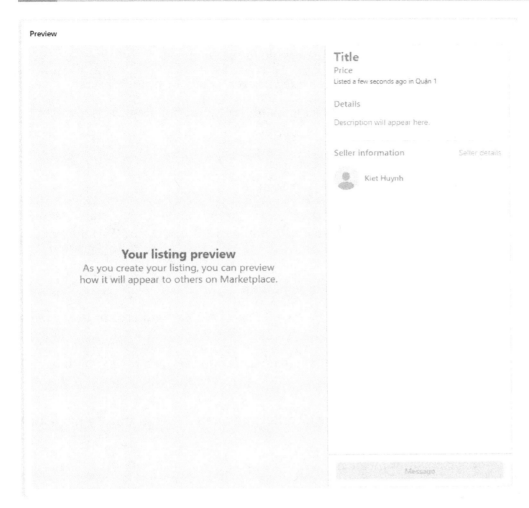

Once you've selected your category, it's time to input all the details about your product. Facebook provides a form with specific fields you need to fill out:

1. Add Photos

- Upload clear and high-quality images of your item. You can add up to **10 photos**, so make use of this to showcase your product from different angles.

- Ensure your images are well-lit and highlight any unique features or details.

- Avoid using heavily edited or stock images; buyers prefer to see the actual condition of the item.

Tips for Taking Good Photos:

- Use natural lighting when possible to avoid harsh shadows.

- Take close-up shots to show details like textures, labels, or brand names.

- Include a scale reference (e.g., placing an object beside the item) if size might be unclear.

2. Title Your Listing

- Write a short, descriptive title for your item.

- Include key details such as the item's brand, model, or main feature. Example: Instead of writing "Phone," use "iPhone 13 Pro Max, 256GB, Like New."

3. Set the Price

- Enter the amount you are asking for your item.

- Be realistic and research similar items on Facebook Marketplace to determine a competitive price.

- Consider adding "OBO" (or best offer) to indicate you are open to negotiation.

4. Choose a Category

- Select the most appropriate category for your item. This ensures your listing appears in relevant searches.

- Examples of categories include:

    o Electronics

    o Home and Garden

    o Clothing and Accessories

    o Sports and Outdoors

5. Describe Your Item

- Provide a detailed and accurate description of your item. Include:

    o **Condition:** New, used, or refurbished.

    o **Specifications:** Dimensions, weight, materials, etc.

- o **Additional Details:** Mention if the item includes accessories, warranties, or manuals.

- o **Honesty:** If there are flaws or damages, describe them to build trust with potential buyers.

Example Description:

"Samsung 55-Inch Smart TV in excellent condition. Model: QLED 4K UHD (2021). Includes remote control and original box. No scratches or damage. Selling because I upgraded to a larger TV."

6. Select Location

- Enter your city or general area to show buyers where the item is located.

- You can adjust the visibility range (e.g., within 10 miles or 50 miles).

7. Set Availability

- Indicate whether the item is available for shipping, local pickup, or both.

- If offering shipping, ensure you understand Facebook's shipping policies and include shipping costs in your pricing.

Step 4: Previewing Your Listing

Before publishing your listing, preview it to ensure all the details are correct. Check:

- Are your photos clear and relevant?

- Is the title accurate and appealing?

- Is the description free of spelling errors?

Take time to make adjustments if necessary. A polished listing will attract more potential buyers.

Step 5: Publishing Your Listing

Once you're satisfied, click **Publish** to post your listing. Facebook will make your item visible to users based on their location and search preferences.

Step 6: Promoting Your Listing (Optional)

To reach a larger audience, you can boost your listing by paying for a **Facebook Ad**. This option is particularly useful if you're selling a high-value item or need to sell quickly.

How to Boost Your Listing:

1. After publishing, select **Boost Listing** from your item's page.

2. Set your budget and duration for the ad campaign.

3. Choose your target audience based on age, location, and interests.

Tips for Crafting a Successful Listing

1. **Be Honest:** Always provide accurate information about your item. Misleading listings can lead to disputes or negative feedback.

2. **Use Keywords:** Think about what buyers might search for and include those terms in your title and description.

3. **Be Responsive:** Reply promptly to messages from potential buyers. Quick responses show professionalism and increase your chances of closing a deal.

4. **Highlight Unique Selling Points:** Mention features that set your item apart, such as being in mint condition, rare availability, or bundled extras.

5. **Offer Flexible Options:** Allowing both local pickup and shipping can attract a broader audience.

Common Mistakes to Avoid

- **Overpricing Your Item:** Research competitors and stay within market rates.

- **Poor-Quality Photos:** Blurry or dark images reduce buyer interest.

- **Incomplete Descriptions:** Missing key details can frustrate buyers and lead to fewer inquiries.

- **Ignoring Messages:** Delayed responses might make buyers lose interest.

Creating an effective listing on Facebook Marketplace is both an art and a science. By investing time and effort into presenting your item clearly and attractively, you increase the likelihood of a quick and successful sale. Always keep your communication professional, follow Facebook's policies, and ensure you're offering a fair deal for both parties. Happy selling!

5.3.3 Communicating with Buyers and Sellers

Facebook Marketplace is a dynamic and interactive platform where buyers and sellers can connect, negotiate, and complete transactions directly within the Facebook ecosystem. To ensure a seamless and safe experience, effective communication is key. This section provides a detailed guide on how to communicate with buyers and sellers on Facebook Marketplace, covering every step of the process.

1. Initiating Communication

When browsing Marketplace listings, if you find an item you're interested in, you can start a conversation with the seller. Conversely, if you are a seller, potential buyers may reach out to inquire about your listing.

For Buyers:

1. **Using the "Message" Button:**

   o When you open a listing, you'll see a "Message" button at the bottom of the item description. Clicking this opens Facebook Messenger, where you can communicate directly with the seller.

   o Start with a polite, concise message, such as:

"Hi, is this item still available? If so, I'm interested and would like to learn more."

   o Avoid vague inquiries like "Still available?" as they may not encourage engagement from the seller.

2. **Customizing Pre-Set Messages:**

- o Facebook offers pre-set messages like "Is this still available?" You can modify these messages to make them more personal. For example:

"Hello, I saw your listing for [item name]. Can you tell me more about its condition?"

3. **Clarity and Purpose:**

- o Clearly state what information you need, such as item dimensions, age, condition, or included accessories. For example:

"Could you let me know if the item comes with all original parts?"

For Sellers:

1. **Responding Promptly:**

- o When a buyer messages you, aim to respond as quickly as possible. Prompt responses create trust and show professionalism.

- o For example, reply with:

"Hi [name], yes, the item is still available. Let me know if you have any specific questions!"

2. **Providing Clear Answers:**

- o Be transparent and concise when answering questions about the item. If the buyer asks for more pictures or details, provide them promptly.

Buyer: "Could you send a closer photo of the product?"
Seller: "Of course! Here's a clearer picture showing the condition."

3. **Being Proactive:**

- o If a buyer seems interested but hasn't followed up, you can gently check in:

"Hi, just wanted to follow up and see if you're still interested in the [item name]. Feel free to ask if you have more questions!"

---

2. Negotiating Price and Terms

Negotiation is common on Facebook Marketplace, but it requires tact and professionalism to reach an agreement that satisfies both parties.

For Buyers:

1. **Starting the Negotiation:**

   o   Begin by politely asking if the seller is open to negotiation. For example:

"Would you consider $50 instead of $60 for the item?"

   o   Avoid lowball offers, as they can offend the seller. A good rule of thumb is to start with an offer slightly below the asking price.

2. **Using Justifications:**

   o   If you're offering a lower price, explain your reasoning. For instance:

"I noticed a small scratch in the photo. Would you accept $45 instead?"

3. **Being Flexible:**

   o   Be open to meeting the seller halfway. If the seller counters your offer, assess whether it's reasonable before declining or accepting.

For Sellers:

1. **Responding to Offers:**

   o   If the buyer makes an offer, respond politely, even if it's below your expected price. For example:

"Thank you for your offer. I was hoping to get closer to $60. Would you consider $55?"

2. **Setting Firm Boundaries:**

   o   If you're not willing to negotiate, make it clear but polite:

"Thank you for your interest, but the price is firm."

3. **Offering Bundle Deals:**

   o   If you're selling multiple items, consider offering discounts for buyers purchasing several items:

"If you're interested in this and [another item], I can offer a discount."

---

3. Sharing Additional Details

Clear and thorough communication is essential to minimize misunderstandings.

For Buyers:

- If you need to know about shipping or pickup details, ask directly:

"Do you offer shipping, or is this for local pickup only?"

- Confirm the condition of the item:

"Are there any scratches or issues I should know about?"

For Sellers:

- Provide all necessary information upfront, such as:

  o Pickup location and time availability

  o Preferred payment methods (e.g., cash, digital payments)

  o Item-specific details, such as warranty or return policies

"The item is available for pickup at [location] after 6 PM. I prefer cash or PayPal payments."

---

4. Arranging the Transaction

Once both parties agree on the price and terms, finalize the transaction details.

1. **Setting Up a Meeting:**

   o Choose a safe, public location to meet. Many communities have "safe exchange zones" near police stations specifically for online transactions.

"Let's meet at the parking lot of [store name] at 3 PM."

   o For home pickups, ensure someone else is present for safety.

2. **Clarifying Payment:**

   o Confirm the payment method before meeting:

"Would you prefer cash or Venmo for payment?"

   o As a seller, avoid accepting checks to minimize the risk of fraud.

3. **Verifying the Item:**

   o As a buyer, inspect the item carefully during the meeting.

- o As a seller, encourage buyers to check the item before completing the transaction:

"Feel free to take a close look at the item before paying."

5. Handling Post-Sale Communication

Even after the sale, maintaining courteous communication is essential.

1. **For Buyers:**

   - o If the item doesn't meet expectations, contact the seller politely:

"Hi, I noticed an issue with the item after bringing it home. Could we discuss this further?"

2. **For Sellers:**

   - o If a buyer is unhappy, try to resolve the issue professionally:

"I'm sorry to hear that. How can I assist you with this?"

6. Tips for Effective Communication

- **Be Professional:** Always use polite language and respond promptly.

- **Avoid Overcommunication:** Keep messages concise and to the point.

- **Stay Safe:** Never share personal details like your address or phone number in initial conversations.

- **Use Messenger Features:** Leverage tools like stickers, location sharing, or file attachments to enhance communication.

By following these steps and best practices, you can ensure clear, respectful, and efficient communication with buyers and sellers on Facebook Marketplace. With proper communication, you'll build trust, avoid misunderstandings, and enjoy a smooth transaction experience.

CHAPTER V
Growing Your Presence on Facebook

6.1 Building a Personal Brand

6.1.1 Sharing Value-Driven Content

Building a personal brand on Facebook starts with sharing value-driven content that resonates with your audience. In a crowded digital space, what sets you apart is the ability to provide information, insights, and inspiration that meet the needs of your followers. This section provides a comprehensive guide to creating and sharing content that strengthens your personal brand, fosters engagement, and establishes your authority in your niche.

1. Understanding Value-Driven Content

Value-driven content is content that offers something meaningful to your audience. It could be educational, entertaining, motivational, or a combination of these. The key is to ensure that every post adds value to your audience's lives, solves a problem, or provides a fresh perspective. Here's how to identify what value-driven content means for your brand:

- **Know Your Audience's Needs:** Before creating content, understand who your audience is and what they're looking for. Use tools like Facebook Insights to analyze the demographics of your followers. Are they interested in industry tips, personal stories, or product reviews? Tailor your content to meet those interests.

- **Define Your Expertise:** Highlight the areas where you excel. Are you a skilled marketer, a travel enthusiast, or a fitness coach? Choose topics that align with your expertise and position yourself as a go-to resource in your field.

- **Stay Relevant:** Keep up with trends in your niche. Whether it's the latest technology, fashion trends, or fitness challenges, aligning your content with what's current keeps your brand fresh and appealing.

2. Types of Value-Driven Content

Here are different types of content that deliver value and build your personal brand:

Educational Content

Educating your audience is a powerful way to establish yourself as an authority in your niche. Examples include:

- **How-To Posts:** Step-by-step guides, such as "How to Create an Effective Facebook Post" or "Tips for Better Time Management."

- **Tutorial Videos:** Record and share videos demonstrating your skills or explaining complex topics in simple terms.

- **Infographics:** Visual content summarizing key data or concepts that are easy to understand and share.

Inspirational Content

Motivate your audience with stories, quotes, and messages that uplift and inspire. Examples:

- **Personal Success Stories:** Share moments where you overcame challenges or achieved a goal.

- **Quotes and Reflections:** Post quotes from industry leaders, books, or your own thoughts that encourage and inspire.

Engaging Content

Create content that invites interaction from your audience. Examples:

- **Polls and Questions:** Ask your audience for their opinions on a topic. For instance, "What's your biggest challenge with time management?"

- **Contests and Giveaways:** Organize activities that encourage sharing and participation, such as "Share your best travel photo for a chance to win!"

Entertaining Content

Engage your audience with lighthearted and fun posts that show a personal side. Examples:

- **Behind-the-Scenes Photos or Videos:** Show a day in your life or behind-the-scenes glimpses of your work.

- **Memes or Jokes:** Share relatable humor that aligns with your brand's tone.

Storytelling Content

Stories are a powerful way to connect emotionally with your audience. Examples include:

- **Customer Testimonials:** Share stories from people who've benefited from your work.

- **Your Journey:** Talk about how you got started in your niche, lessons you've learned, and milestones you've achieved.

---

3. Creating High-Quality Content

To maximize the impact of your content, it must be visually appealing, well-crafted, and authentic. Here are some tips for creating high-quality posts:

Focus on Visuals

Visual content is more likely to capture attention.

- Use high-resolution images that align with your brand's theme.

- Incorporate branding elements like your logo or colors in your visuals.

- Create professional-looking graphics using tools like Canva.

Write Compelling Captions

Your captions should provide context, spark curiosity, or encourage interaction.

- Use clear and concise language.

- Start with a hook to grab attention. For example, "Did you know that 70% of businesses grow their audience using Facebook?"

- End with a call-to-action (CTA), such as "Comment below with your thoughts!" or "Share this post if you found it helpful."

Use Consistent Branding

Your content should reflect a consistent style, tone, and message.

- Define your brand's voice—whether it's professional, casual, or motivational.
- Stick to a consistent posting schedule to maintain visibility.

4. Sharing Content Strategically

Sharing content effectively means knowing when, where, and how to post for maximum impact.

Timing is Key

Post when your audience is most active. Use Facebook Insights to determine peak engagement times and schedule posts accordingly.

Leverage Facebook Features

- Use **Stories** to share quick, engaging updates that disappear after 24 hours.
- Pin important posts to the top of your profile for better visibility.
- Use **Reels** for short, engaging video content that has high reach potential.

Engage Consistently

Posting is only half the battle; engaging with your audience is equally important.

- Reply to comments on your posts to build relationships.
- Thank your audience for their support and acknowledge their contributions.
- Participate in discussions within groups and communities related to your niche.

5. Measuring Success

Finally, measure the effectiveness of your content to understand what works and what doesn't.

Track Engagement Metrics

Use tools like Facebook Insights to monitor:

- Likes, comments, and shares on your posts.

- Reach and impressions to see how many people your content is reaching.

- Click-through rates for links shared in your posts.

Experiment and Adapt

Not every post will perform the same way, so test different types of content to see what resonates best. Adjust your strategy based on audience feedback and performance data.

---

6. Conclusion

Sharing value-driven content is the cornerstone of building a personal brand on Facebook. By focusing on creating content that educates, inspires, engages, and entertains, you can establish trust and loyalty with your audience. Pair this with consistent posting, strategic engagement, and regular analysis, and you'll be well on your way to becoming a recognizable and respected figure in your niche.

6.1.2 Engaging with Your Audience

Building a personal brand on Facebook requires more than just sharing content—it demands meaningful engagement with your audience. Engaging effectively helps you foster trust, create stronger connections, and establish a loyal following. In this section, we'll explore how to engage with your audience in a thoughtful and strategic way, covering techniques, tools, and best practices.

---

1. Understanding the Importance of Engagement

Engagement is the foundation of building relationships on Facebook. Without it, your posts, no matter how high-quality, can easily get lost in the algorithm. Facebook prioritizes content that sparks meaningful conversations and interactions. Therefore, when you engage with your audience, you not only build rapport but also boost the visibility of your posts.

Key benefits of audience engagement include:

- Building trust and credibility.

- Encouraging followers to share your content.

- Turning casual followers into loyal supporters.

- Increasing organic reach through the Facebook algorithm.

2. Responding to Comments and Messages

One of the simplest and most effective ways to engage your audience is by responding to their comments and messages. This shows that you value their input and appreciate their time.

How to Respond Effectively:

- **Be Timely:** Respond as quickly as possible. Facebook tracks response times, and a fast response rate improves your profile's credibility.

- **Be Personable:** Address users by name where possible and adopt a friendly, conversational tone.

- **Acknowledge Positive Feedback:** If someone leaves a positive comment, thank them and continue the conversation with a follow-up question.

- **Handle Negative Comments with Grace:** Respond professionally to criticism or complaints, offering solutions where possible. Avoid defensiveness.

Pro Tip: Use Facebook's **Auto-Reply** feature to acknowledge messages instantly and let people know you'll get back to them soon.

3. Creating Interactive Content

Interactive content is a powerful way to spark discussions and keep your audience engaged. People are more likely to interact with posts that invite their opinions, questions, or participation.

Types of Interactive Content:

- **Polls and Surveys:** Use Facebook's polling feature to ask questions about your audience's preferences or opinions. Example: *"What type of content would you like to see more of on this page?"*

- **Questions and Prompts:** Post open-ended questions to encourage meaningful responses. Example: *"What's the best piece of advice you've received in your career?"*

- **Quizzes and Games:** Create light-hearted challenges or trivia related to your niche.

- **Live Videos:** Host live Q&A sessions to engage directly with your followers in real-time. Encourage viewers to comment and ask questions during the session.

Best Practices for Interactive Content:

- Tailor content to your audience's interests and needs.

- Keep your tone friendly and approachable.

- Follow up with comments and reactions to show you value participants' input.

4. Using Reactions and Emojis

Facebook offers a variety of reaction buttons, including Like, Love, Haha, Wow, Sad, and Angry. These allow users to express how they feel about your content quickly. Engaging with these reactions can help deepen your connection with your audience.

How to Leverage Reactions:

- React to your followers' comments and posts to show appreciation or agreement.

- Use emojis in your posts to make them more relatable and visually appealing.

- Encourage your audience to react. For example: *"Tap the ❤️ if you agree!"*

5. Encouraging User-Generated Content (UGC)

User-generated content is a fantastic way to engage your audience and build community. When your followers create content about your brand or niche and share it, it boosts your credibility and reach.

Strategies to Encourage UGC:

- **Create Challenges or Campaigns:** Ask your followers to share photos or videos related to a specific theme or hashtag. Example: *"Share a photo of your workspace using #MyCreativeDesk!"*

- **Feature Followers' Content:** Highlight user-generated content on your page to show appreciation. This also motivates others to contribute.

- **Run Contests:** Host contests where participants submit content to win prizes. Example: *"Share your favorite recipe with us for a chance to win a gift card!"*

Pro Tip: Always seek permission before reposting user-generated content.

6. Building a Community Through Groups

Creating a Facebook Group related to your niche allows you to foster a sense of community among your followers. Groups are ideal for encouraging discussions, sharing advice, and building deeper connections.

Steps to Build an Engaged Group:

1. **Define the Purpose:** Clearly outline what your group is about and the type of members you want to attract.

2. **Set Rules:** Establish group guidelines to maintain a positive and respectful environment.

3. **Share Valuable Content:** Post consistently and offer content that sparks conversation or solves problems.

4. **Moderate Actively:** Ensure discussions stay on track and address inappropriate behavior quickly.

Tips for Group Engagement:

- Host weekly threads to encourage participation, such as "Question of the Week" or "Share Your Wins."

- Tag members in posts to encourage them to join discussions.

- Recognize active contributors by highlighting their input.

7. Hosting Facebook Live Sessions

Facebook Live is one of the most engaging formats on the platform. It allows you to interact directly with your audience in real-time, building authenticity and trust.

Ideas for Live Sessions:

- Answer frequently asked questions.

- Share behind-the-scenes looks at your work or life.

- Host interviews with other experts in your niche.

- Teach a skill or provide a tutorial.

Best Practices for Live Sessions:

- Announce your live session ahead of time to maximize attendance.

- Interact with viewers by addressing them by name and answering their questions.

- Keep your energy high and maintain a conversational tone.

---

8. Monitoring and Adapting Your Engagement Strategy

Engagement is not a one-size-fits-all process. To ensure success, you must analyze your efforts and adapt based on your audience's preferences.

Metrics to Track:

- **Engagement Rate:** Monitor likes, comments, shares, and reactions to measure how your audience interacts with your content.

- **Post Reach:** Assess how many people your posts are reaching organically.

- **Message Response Rate:** Check how quickly you're responding to messages.

Tools to Use:

- **Facebook Insights:** Offers detailed analytics about your page performance.

- **Third-Party Tools:** Platforms like Hootsuite and Buffer can help you monitor and manage engagement across multiple platforms.

9. Staying Authentic

Above all, authenticity is the key to effective engagement. People are drawn to genuine interactions, so let your personality shine through in your content and responses.

Tips for Authenticity:

- Be transparent about your goals and values.

- Share personal stories or experiences that your audience can relate to.

- Admit mistakes when they happen and show how you've learned from them.

By following these strategies, you can foster deeper connections with your audience and grow your personal brand on Facebook effectively. Engagement isn't just about numbers—it's about building meaningful relationships that make your presence stand out.

6.2 Facebook for Small Businesses

6.2.1 Creating a Business Page

Introduction

A Facebook Business Page is an essential tool for small businesses to establish an online presence, connect with customers, and grow their brand. Unlike personal profiles, Business Pages offer features specifically designed for companies, such as analytics, advertising options, and customer interaction tools.

In this section, we will walk you through the step-by-step process of creating a Facebook Business Page, including how to optimize it for visibility and engagement. By the end of this chapter, you will have a fully functional Facebook Page that reflects your brand and attracts potential customers.

Step 1: Understanding the Benefits of a Facebook Business Page

Before we dive into the setup process, let's explore the key benefits of having a Facebook Business Page:

- **Increased Online Presence:** A Business Page provides a professional space where customers can find information about your products, services, and company updates.

- **Customer Engagement:** You can interact with followers through posts, messages, and comments, building stronger relationships with your audience.

- **Insights and Analytics:** Facebook provides built-in tools to track engagement, audience demographics, and post performance.

- **Advertising Opportunities:** With a Business Page, you can run targeted Facebook ads to reach a specific audience.

- **SEO Benefits:** A well-optimized Facebook Business Page can appear in search engine results, increasing your brand's discoverability.

Step 2: Setting Up Your Facebook Business Page

2.1 Logging Into Facebook

To create a Business Page, you need a personal Facebook account. If you don't have one, you must first sign up at Facebook.com.

Once logged in, follow these steps:

1. Click on the menu button (three horizontal lines) in the top right corner of the screen.

2. Select **"Pages"** from the dropdown menu.

3. Click **"Create New Page."**

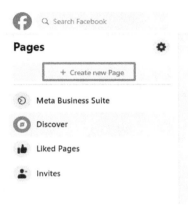

2.2 Choosing the Right Page Name and Category

Your Page name should be the same as your business name or a recognizable variation of it.

- **Example:** If your business is "Bella's Bakery," your Page name should be **Bella's Bakery** rather than something unclear like "Best Cakes in Town."

Next, choose a category that best describes your business. Facebook allows you to select up to three categories.

Common Business Page Categories:

- **Retail:** Clothing Store, Electronics Store, Bookstore

- **Food & Beverage:** Restaurant, Café, Bakery

- **Professional Services:** Consulting Agency, Digital Marketing Agency, Financial Services

- **Health & Wellness:** Gym, Yoga Studio, Personal Trainer

Once you've selected a category, add a short **business description** (up to 255 characters). This should briefly explain what your business does.

- **Example:** "Bella's Bakery offers handcrafted cakes, pastries, and desserts made with high-quality ingredients. Visit us for freshly baked treats daily!"

Step 3: Adding Essential Business Information

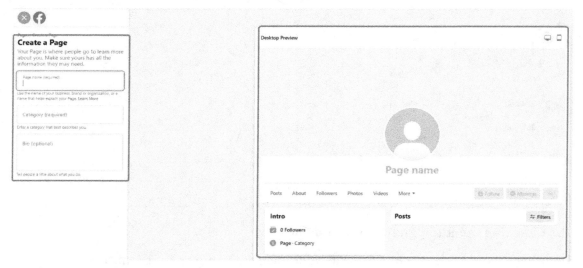

3.1 Uploading a Profile Picture and Cover Photo

Your profile picture should be a clear representation of your brand. For most businesses, this is typically:

- **Your logo** (recommended size: 170x170 pixels).

- **A recognizable brand symbol or mascot.**

The **cover photo** should visually represent your brand's identity. Ideal options include:

- A high-quality image of your store or products.

- A promotional banner showcasing discounts or upcoming events.

- A branded background with your slogan.

Recommended cover photo size: 820x312 pixels.

3.2 Adding Contact Information

Make it easy for customers to reach you by adding essential contact details:

- **Website URL** (if applicable).

- **Phone number** (if you offer customer service via phone).

- **Business email address.**

- **Physical address** (if you have a physical location).

- **Operating hours** (especially important for restaurants and retail stores).

Step 4: Customizing Your Facebook Page

4.1 Adding an Action Button

Facebook allows you to add a **Call-to-Action (CTA) button** to encourage customers to take action. Popular options include:

- **Book Now** – Ideal for appointment-based businesses.

- **Shop Now** – Directs users to your online store.

- **Call Now** – Lets customers call your business directly.

- **Send Message** – Encourages direct communication via Messenger.

To add a CTA button:

1. Click the **"+ Add a Button"** option under your cover photo.

2. Choose the appropriate action for your business.

3. Follow the on-screen instructions to complete the setup.

4.2 Completing the "About" Section

The **About** section is where visitors learn more about your business. It should include:

- **A detailed business description:** This can be longer than the short bio added earlier.

- **Mission statement:** Share what your company stands for.

- **Company history:** If your business has a compelling story, include it.

4.3 Setting Up Page Tabs

Facebook offers customizable tabs that help organize content. The most commonly used tabs include:

- **Home** – Displays your latest posts and business information.

- **Shop** – Allows businesses to list and sell products directly on Facebook.

- **Services** – Ideal for businesses offering specific services.

- **Reviews** – Displays customer feedback and ratings.

- **Photos & Videos** – Showcases media content related to your business.

To customize tabs:

1. Go to **"Settings"** > **"Templates and Tabs."**

2. Rearrange or add/remove tabs based on your business needs.

Step 5: Publishing Your First Post

Once your Page is set up, it's time to make your first post. Here are some ideas for your initial content:

- **A welcome message:** Introduce your business and what customers can expect.

- **Behind-the-scenes photos:** Show how your products are made.

- **Customer testimonials:** Highlight positive reviews from existing customers.

- **Special promotions:** Announce exclusive deals or discounts.

To publish a post:

1. Click the **"Create Post"** button.

2. Write your content, add images/videos, and include relevant hashtags.

3. Click **"Post"** to share it with your audience.

Step 6: Inviting People to Like Your Page

Now that your Page is live, you need followers! Here's how to start growing your audience:

- **Invite friends and family:** Click the **"Invite Friends"** button to send invitations.

- **Promote on other platforms:** Share your Facebook link on your website, Instagram, and email newsletters.

- **Encourage customers to follow:** Ask satisfied customers to like and review your Page.

Conclusion

Creating a Facebook Business Page is a crucial step for any small business looking to establish an online presence. By following these steps, you can set up a professional and engaging Page that attracts customers and grows your brand.

In the next section, we'll explore **Facebook Insights** and how to analyze your Page's performance to maximize engagement and reach.

6.2.2 Understanding Facebook Insights

Facebook Insights is a powerful analytics tool designed to help small businesses track and measure their performance on Facebook. By using Insights, you can understand how your audience interacts with your content, which posts perform best, and how to optimize your strategy to grow your presence on the platform.

In this section, we will cover everything you need to know about Facebook Insights, including how to access it, the key metrics you should track, and how to use this data to improve your business's performance.

1. What is Facebook Insights?

Facebook Insights is a free analytics tool that provides detailed data about how your business page is performing. It gives you information on post engagement, audience demographics, page reach, and other important metrics. By analyzing these insights, you can make informed decisions to optimize your content strategy and grow your business.

For small businesses, Facebook Insights is crucial because it helps you:

- Understand who your audience is and what content they engage with.

- Track your page's growth over time.

- Identify the best times to post for maximum engagement.

- Measure the effectiveness of paid advertisements.

2. How to Access Facebook Insights

To access Facebook Insights, follow these steps:

1. Log into your Facebook Business Page.

2. On the left-hand menu, find and click on **"Insights"** (or **"Professional Dashboard"** in some layouts).

3. You will be directed to the main **Facebook Insights dashboard**, where you can see an overview of key metrics.

Alternatively, if you are using **Meta Business Suite**, you can go to **Meta Business Suite > Insights** to get even more detailed analytics.

3. Key Metrics in Facebook Insights

Facebook Insights provides a wealth of data, but as a small business owner, focusing on the most important metrics will help you make strategic decisions without feeling overwhelmed.

3.1 Overview Metrics

When you open Facebook Insights, the first thing you will see is an overview of your page's performance. This includes:

- **Page Likes and Follows** – The number of people who have liked or followed your page.

- **Reach** – The total number of unique users who have seen your content.

- **Engagement** – The number of interactions (likes, comments, shares) your posts have received.

- **Post Performance** – A summary of how your recent posts are performing.

3.2 Post Reach and Engagement

One of the most critical aspects of Facebook Insights is understanding how far your content reaches and how people interact with it.

- **Post Reach** – This tells you how many unique users have seen your posts. There are two types:

  - **Organic Reach** – The number of people who saw your content naturally, without paid promotion.

  - **Paid Reach** – The number of people who saw your content due to a paid Facebook ad.

- **Post Engagement** – Measures how many people interacted with your post. This includes:

  - **Reactions (Likes, Love, Wow, etc.)**

  - **Comments**

  - **Shares**

  - **Clicks (on links, images, or videos)**

A high engagement rate means that your content is resonating with your audience, which helps boost your organic reach due to Facebook's algorithm favoring engaging posts.

3.3 Audience Insights

Knowing who your audience is can help you tailor your content to better suit their interests. Facebook Insights provides data on:

- **Demographics** – Age, gender, and location of your followers.

- **Top Cities & Countries** – Where most of your audience is from.

- **Active Hours & Days** – The times and days when your followers are most active on Facebook.

By understanding these metrics, you can adjust your posting schedule and content strategy to better reach your target audience.

3.4 Page Likes and Followers Growth

Tracking your **Page Likes** and **Followers Growth** can help you understand how well your business is attracting new audiences.

- **Net Followers** – The total number of people who followed your page minus those who unfollowed.

- **Sources of Likes** – Shows where your new followers came from (e.g., organic discovery, ads, page recommendations).

- **Follower Trends** – Helps you see if there are specific events, posts, or campaigns that triggered an increase in followers.

If you notice a sudden drop in followers, review your recent posts and engagement to identify what might have caused it.

3.5 Video Performance (If Applicable)

If your business uses videos on Facebook, you can track:

- **Video Views** – How many times your video has been watched.

- **3-Second Views** – The number of users who watched at least three seconds of your video.

- **Average Watch Time** – The average amount of time viewers spent watching your videos.

This data helps you understand whether your videos are engaging and if you need to adjust your content to keep viewers watching longer.

4. How to Use Facebook Insights to Improve Your Business

Now that you understand the key metrics, here are some practical ways to use this data to improve your business's Facebook strategy.

4.1 Optimize Your Posting Schedule

By analyzing **Active Hours & Days**, you can determine the best times to post for maximum engagement. Try scheduling your posts during peak hours when your audience is most active.

4.2 Identify Top-Performing Content

Check which posts have the highest engagement. Are they videos, images, or text posts? Do they include questions, promotions, or storytelling? Once you identify what works best, create more of that type of content.

4.3 Adjust Your Advertising Strategy

If you're running Facebook ads, use **Paid Reach & Engagement** metrics to see which ads perform best. Adjust your targeting, budget, and creative elements based on the insights to get better results.

4.4 Improve Audience Targeting

Use **Demographics & Locations** data to tailor your content to better fit your audience's preferences. If most of your audience is from a specific region, consider creating localized content.

4.5 Experiment with Content Formats

If you notice that videos are performing better than text posts, consider incorporating more video content. Facebook favors video content in its algorithm, so this could help increase your reach.

4.6 Track Progress and Adjust Accordingly

Regularly check Facebook Insights to monitor progress and adjust your strategy. Set goals for your business (e.g., increasing engagement by 20% in three months) and track your performance over time.

5. Conclusion

Facebook Insights is a powerful tool that helps small businesses understand their audience, improve engagement, and optimize their marketing strategies. By regularly analyzing and acting on the data provided by Insights, you can grow your Facebook presence and maximize your business potential.

To summarize, here's what you should focus on:

✓ **Monitor your reach and engagement regularly**
✓ **Post at the best times for your audience**
✓ **Analyze your top-performing content and create more of it**
✓ **Use audience insights to tailor your messaging**
✓ **Adjust your Facebook ad strategy based on performance data**

By leveraging Facebook Insights effectively, your small business can build a stronger social media presence, connect with the right audience, and ultimately drive more success on the platform.

6.3 Running Facebook Ads

6.3.1 Setting Up an Ad Campaign

Running Facebook Ads can be a powerful way to reach new audiences, promote products or services, and grow your brand. However, setting up a successful ad campaign requires careful planning and an understanding of Facebook's advertising tools. In this section, we will go through the step-by-step process of setting up a Facebook ad campaign, from defining objectives to launching your ad.

1. Understanding Facebook Ad Campaign Structure

Before creating an ad campaign, it's important to understand the three levels of Facebook advertising:

1. **Campaign Level** – This is where you set your overall advertising objective, such as brand awareness, website traffic, or conversions.

2. **Ad Set Level** – Here, you define your audience, budget, schedule, and ad placements.

3. **Ad Level** – This is where you create the actual ad, including images, videos, headlines, and call-to-action buttons.

Each level plays a crucial role in the effectiveness of your ad campaign, so you need to configure them carefully to achieve your goals.

2. Choosing the Right Campaign Objective

The first step in setting up a Facebook ad campaign is selecting your campaign objective. Facebook provides several objectives categorized into three main groups:

Awareness Objectives (For reaching more people)

- **Brand Awareness** – Increase recognition of your brand among potential customers.

- **Reach** – Show your ad to as many people as possible within your target audience.

Consideration Objectives (For engaging with potential customers)

- **Traffic** – Drive users to a website, landing page, or app.

- **Engagement** – Increase likes, shares, and comments on your posts.

- **App Installs** – Encourage users to download your mobile app.

- **Video Views** – Promote videos to a larger audience.

- **Lead Generation** – Collect potential customers' information through forms.

- **Messages** – Start conversations with customers through Messenger, Instagram DM, or WhatsApp.

Conversion Objectives (For driving sales and actions)

- **Conversions** – Encourage users to take a specific action, such as making a purchase or signing up.

- **Catalog Sales** – Promote products from your online store.

- **Store Traffic** – Drive visitors to your physical store locations.

Choosing the right objective is critical because Facebook will optimize your ads based on your chosen goal.

---

3. Setting Up a New Facebook Ad Campaign

Step 1: Accessing Facebook Ads Manager

1. Log in to your **Facebook Business Manager**.

2. Click on **"Ads Manager"** from the left-hand menu.

3. Click the **"Create"** button to start a new campaign.

Step 2: Selecting a Campaign Objective

- Choose the objective that aligns with your goals (refer to section 2).

- Click **"Continue"** to move to the campaign setup screen.

Step 3: Naming Your Campaign and Setting a Budget

- Give your campaign a clear and descriptive name. Example: **"Summer Sale - Traffic Campaign"**.

- Toggle **A/B Testing** on if you want to test different ad variations.

- Choose whether you want **Advantage Campaign Budget** (Facebook automatically optimizes budget across ad sets) or set budgets manually at the ad set level.

Step 4: Selecting Special Categories (If Applicable)

- If your ad relates to housing, employment, credit, social issues, elections, or politics, you must declare it as a **Special Ad Category** to comply with Facebook's policies.

Step 5: Setting Up Campaign Bidding Strategy

- Choose a **bidding strategy**:

  - **Lowest Cost** – Facebook will get you the most results for your budget.

  - **Cost Cap** – You set a maximum amount you're willing to pay per action.

After configuring these settings, click **"Next"** to move to the ad set level.

---

4. Configuring the Ad Set

Step 1: Defining Your Target Audience

At the ad set level, you define your **target audience**, which determines who will see your ad. There are several targeting options:

Demographic Targeting

- **Location** – Target users based on country, city, or radius around a specific area.

- **Age and Gender** – Define the age range and gender of your ideal audience.

- **Languages** – Target users who speak a specific language.

Interest-Based Targeting

- Target users based on their interests, behaviors, and online activity (e.g., fitness, technology, travel, fashion).

Custom Audiences & Lookalike Audiences

- **Custom Audiences** – Retarget people who have interacted with your website, app, or Facebook page.

- **Lookalike Audiences** – Find new people similar to your existing customers.

Step 2: Setting Budget and Schedule

- **Daily Budget** – Facebook will spend up to this amount each day.

- **Lifetime Budget** – Facebook will distribute your budget over a set period.

- **Schedule** – Choose whether to run the ad **continuously** or **on specific dates**.

Step 3: Choosing Ad Placements

- **Automatic Placements** – Facebook decides where to show your ads for the best results.

- **Manual Placements** – You can select specific placements such as:
    - Facebook Feed
    - Instagram Feed
    - Facebook Stories
    - Instagram Stories
    - Messenger
    - Audience Network

Once your ad set is configured, click **"Next"** to move to the ad creation level.

---

5. Creating the Ad

Step 1: Selecting the Ad Format

Choose the format that best suits your campaign goal:

- **Single Image or Video** – Display one image or video.

- **Carousel** – Show multiple images or videos in one ad.

- **Collection** – A mobile-friendly format for e-commerce.

Step 2: Adding Creative Elements

- **Upload Images or Videos** – Use high-quality visuals that align with your brand.

- **Write a Compelling Primary Text** – Clearly explain what your ad is about.

- **Add a Headline** – Create a catchy, attention-grabbing headline.

- **Choose a Call-to-Action (CTA) Button** – Examples: "Learn More," "Shop Now," "Sign Up."

Step 3: Setting the Destination URL

- If you want users to visit your website, enter the correct landing page link.

- Ensure your website is **mobile-friendly** to maximize conversions.

Step 4: Previewing and Testing Your Ad

- Use the preview tool to check how your ad looks on different placements.

- Test different versions of the ad to see which performs best (A/B testing).

6. Launching and Monitoring Your Campaign

Step 1: Reviewing Your Campaign

- Check all settings and ensure everything is correct.

- Click **"Publish"** to launch your campaign.

Step 2: Monitoring Ad Performance

- Go to **Ads Manager** and track metrics such as:

    o   Impressions

    o   Click-through rate (CTR)

    o   Conversion rate

    o   Cost per result (CPR)

- Use **Facebook Ads Insights** to analyze which ad variations are performing best and make adjustments if needed.

Conclusion

Setting up a Facebook ad campaign requires strategic planning, from choosing the right objective to targeting the right audience and crafting compelling ad creatives. By following this guide, you can create a well-optimized ad campaign that maximizes your budget and achieves your business goals. In the next section, we will explore how to refine your targeting strategy to reach the right audience efficiently.

6.3.2 Targeting the Right Audience

Facebook Ads provide an incredibly powerful way to reach the right audience for your business, ensuring your ads appear in front of people who are most likely to engage, click, or convert. However, the success of your Facebook ad campaign depends largely on how well you define and target your audience.

In this section, we'll explore how to set up precise audience targeting using Facebook's tools, including demographic segmentation, interest-based targeting, custom audiences, and lookalike audiences. By the end, you'll have a clear understanding of how to refine your ad strategy to maximize effectiveness.

1. Why Targeting Matters in Facebook Ads

Targeting the right audience is crucial because:

- **It increases engagement and conversion rates** – Showing ads to people genuinely interested in your product or service means higher chances of clicks and purchases.

- **It helps you control ad spending** – Precise targeting ensures that your budget isn't wasted on people who are unlikely to take action.

- **It improves ad relevance and quality score** – Facebook rewards well-targeted ads with lower costs per result, improving your return on investment (ROI).

2. Audience Targeting Options in Facebook Ads

Facebook provides multiple audience targeting options, allowing you to reach users based on different characteristics and behaviors.

2.1 Core Audience Targeting (Demographics & Interests)

The Core Audience feature lets you define your target market based on basic but essential factors such as:

a. Location Targeting

You can target people based on their:

- **Country, state, city, or zip code** – Ideal for businesses serving specific locations.
- **Radius targeting** – Allows you to target users within a custom radius around a particular address (great for local businesses).
- **Travel behavior** – Choose between "People living in this location," "People recently in this location," or "People traveling in this location."

b. Age and Gender Targeting

- Define the age range of your audience (e.g., 18-24, 25-34, 35-44, etc.).
- Select specific genders if your product or service caters to a particular group.

c. Interest-Based Targeting

Facebook collects data from user interactions (likes, follows, clicks, searches) to categorize interests. You can target users based on:

- **Hobbies and activities** – Sports, fitness, photography, etc.
- **Entertainment preferences** – Music, movies, TV shows, etc.
- **Shopping behavior** – Online buyers, frequent shoppers, brand preferences.
- **Industry and profession** – Business owners, IT professionals, teachers, etc.

d. Behavioral Targeting

Facebook tracks user behavior, allowing advertisers to target based on:

- **Purchase behavior** – Recent buyers, frequent spenders.
- **Device usage** – Android users, iPhone users.

- **Travel habits** – Frequent travelers, international travelers.

2.2 Custom Audiences (Retargeting & Engagement-Based Targeting)

Custom Audiences allow you to target people who have already interacted with your business in some way. This is useful for **retargeting** campaigns, where you re-engage people who visited your website or engaged with your Facebook page.

Here's how to create and use Custom Audiences:

a. Website Custom Audience

- Use **Facebook Pixel** to track visitors who landed on your website.
- Target users who browsed a specific product page but didn't purchase.
- Retarget people who abandoned their shopping cart.

b. Customer List Custom Audience

- Upload a list of customer emails or phone numbers (from your CRM).
- Facebook will match these contacts to their profiles and show them your ads.
- Great for loyalty programs, VIP offers, and personalized promotions.

c. Engagement Custom Audience

- Target users who interacted with your Facebook page, Instagram profile, or watched a video ad.
- Set up **video retargeting** for people who watched at least 50% of your video ad.
- Target users who previously messaged your Facebook page.

2.3 Lookalike Audiences (Expanding Your Reach)

Lookalike Audiences allow you to find **new people** who share similar traits and behaviors with your existing customers. Facebook analyzes your Custom Audience and identifies similar users.

a. How to Create a Lookalike Audience

1. Choose a source audience (your best-performing customers, engaged users, or email list).

2. Select a **percentage match** (1%-10% similarity).

   o **1% Lookalike** – Closest match, smaller but high-quality audience.

   o **10% Lookalike** – Larger audience, broader but less precise targeting.

3. Choose the target country where you want to find similar people.

b. Best Practices for Lookalike Audiences

- Use **high-quality source data** – Choose customers who have completed purchases rather than random website visitors.

- Combine with **interest-based filters** – Narrow down Lookalike Audiences further by adding interests and behaviors.

- Avoid overlap – Use **Audience Overlap Tool** to prevent targeting the same people in multiple campaigns.

3. Advanced Audience Targeting Strategies

3.1 Layering Multiple Targeting Methods

- Combine demographic filters with interest-based targeting.

- Use Custom Audiences for warm leads and Lookalike Audiences for new prospects.

- Apply behavior filters to refine your audience (e.g., frequent online shoppers + engaged video viewers).

3.2 Excluding Irrelevant Audiences

Exclusions help improve ad efficiency by avoiding wasteful spending.

- **Exclude existing customers** if the ad is for new leads.

- **Exclude past buyers** if promoting an introductory offer.

- **Exclude low-engagement users** if focusing on high-value interactions.

3.3 A/B Testing Audience Segments

Test different targeting options to see which performs best.

- Run **separate campaigns** for different age groups or locations.
- Compare broad targeting vs. Lookalike Audiences.
- Adjust based on ad performance and engagement metrics.

4. Measuring and Optimizing Audience Performance

4.1 Tracking Audience Engagement in Facebook Ads Manager

- Monitor metrics such as **CTR (Click-Through Rate), CPC (Cost per Click), and ROAS (Return on Ad Spend).**
- Identify which audience segments are generating the most conversions.

4.2 Adjusting Targeting Based on Data Insights

- If engagement is **low**, refine interests or behaviors.
- If conversions are **high**, scale up your budget for that audience.
- If CPC is **too high**, test different Lookalike Audiences or broaden targeting.

5. Conclusion

Targeting the right audience is one of the most critical aspects of running successful Facebook Ads. By leveraging demographic filters, interest-based targeting, Custom Audiences, and Lookalike Audiences, you can ensure your ads reach the right people at the right time.

To maximize success:

✓ Define your audience precisely using Facebook's built-in tools.
✓ Retarget past visitors and engaged users to improve conversions.
✓ Use Lookalike Audiences to expand your reach efficiently.
✓ Continuously analyze and adjust your targeting for optimal results.

Mastering audience targeting will help you create **high-performing Facebook ad campaigns** that drive meaningful engagement and business growth.

6.3.3 Analyzing Ad Performance

Running Facebook Ads is an essential tool for businesses and individuals looking to expand their reach. However, launching an ad campaign is only the first step. To ensure that your ads are effective, you need to analyze their performance carefully. Facebook provides a comprehensive set of tools that help you measure the impact of your campaigns and make data-driven decisions. This section will guide you through the key performance indicators (KPIs), how to interpret Facebook Ads Manager reports, and how to optimize your ads based on data insights.

1. Understanding Key Performance Indicators (KPIs)

Before analyzing your ad performance, you need to understand the most critical metrics. Facebook Ads Manager provides a wealth of data, but not every metric is relevant to your specific goals. Below are some key performance indicators to focus on:

Reach and Impressions

- **Reach**: The total number of unique users who saw your ad at least once.

- **Impressions**: The total number of times your ad was displayed, including multiple views by the same user.

- **Frequency**: The average number of times each person saw your ad (Impressions ÷ Reach).

- **Why it matters**: High reach means your ad is being seen by many users, but if the frequency is too high, it may indicate ad fatigue, where users see the same ad too often and start ignoring it.

Engagement Metrics

- **Clicks**: The total number of times users clicked on your ad.

- **Click-Through Rate (CTR)**: The percentage of people who saw your ad and clicked on it (Clicks ÷ Impressions × 100).

- **Reactions, Comments, and Shares**: These indicate user interactions with your ad.

- **Why it matters**: A high CTR means your ad is compelling and relevant to your audience. Low engagement might indicate that the ad needs to be more appealing or better targeted.

Conversion Metrics

- **Conversions**: The number of users who completed the desired action (e.g., signing up, making a purchase).

- **Cost per Conversion (CPC or CPA - Cost Per Action)**: The average amount you spent to get one conversion.

- **Return on Ad Spend (ROAS)**: The revenue generated compared to the amount spent on the ad.

- **Why it matters**: These metrics help you determine if your ads are driving actual business results. A low ROAS might mean that your ad needs better targeting or optimization.

Video Ad Metrics (if using video ads)

- **Video Views**: The number of times your video was watched for at least 3 seconds.

- **Average Watch Time**: The average amount of time people spend watching your video.

- **Completion Rate**: The percentage of users who watched your video until the end.

- **Why it matters**: If users are not watching the full video, consider making it shorter or more engaging in the first few seconds.

---

2. Using Facebook Ads Manager for Performance Analysis

Facebook Ads Manager is the primary tool for tracking ad performance. Here's how to navigate and interpret the data:

Accessing Ads Manager Reports

1. Log into Facebook and go to **Ads Manager**.

2. Click on the **Campaigns**, **Ad Sets**, or **Ads** tab, depending on the level you want to analyze.

3. Use the **Columns** dropdown to select different report views (e.g., Performance, Engagement, Conversions).

4. Apply filters and date ranges to compare performance over time.

Understanding Ads Manager Dashboard

- **Overview Tab**: Provides a summary of ad performance, including spend, impressions, and engagement.

- **Breakdown Feature**: Allows you to analyze performance by demographics, devices, placements, and locations.

- **Graphs and Trends**: Helps you visualize data and spot trends in performance.

Customizing Reports for Better Insights

1. Click on **Customize Columns** to choose the most relevant metrics.

2. Save reports for future reference by clicking **Save Report**.

3. Export data for deeper analysis using Excel or Google Sheets.

3. Optimizing Ads Based on Performance Data

Once you have analyzed your ad performance, the next step is optimization. Here's how you can make data-driven improvements:

Improving Click-Through Rate (CTR)

- **Enhance Ad Creative**: Use high-quality images, videos, and compelling copy.

- **Refine Your Headline**: Make it clear, engaging, and benefit-driven.

- **Use Strong Call-to-Action (CTA)**: Encourage users to take the desired action (e.g., "Sign Up Now," "Shop Today").

Reducing Cost per Click (CPC)

- **Narrow Your Audience**: Target users who are more likely to be interested in your product or service.

- **Adjust Bidding Strategy**: Experiment with different bid amounts and see which one gives you the best results.

- **Improve Landing Page Experience**: Make sure the page users land on is relevant, fast-loading, and user-friendly.

Increasing Conversions

- **Use Retargeting Ads**: Show ads to users who have previously interacted with your brand.

- **Optimize for Mobile Users**: Ensure that your website and ad content are mobile-friendly.

- **Test Different Offers**: Experiment with discounts, limited-time deals, or free trials to encourage conversions.

Preventing Ad Fatigue

- **Rotate Ad Creatives**: Change images, videos, and copy regularly.

- **Adjust Audience Segments**: Exclude users who have already converted.

- **Use Frequency Capping**: Limit how often an individual sees your ad.

---

4. A/B Testing for Continuous Improvement

A/B testing (also known as split testing) is essential for optimizing ad performance. Here's how to conduct effective tests:

What to Test?

- **Ad Creative**: Compare different images, videos, or colors.

- **Ad Copy**: Test variations in wording, tone, and CTAs.

- **Audience Targeting**: Experiment with different demographics, interests, and behaviors.

- **Placements**: Test ads in different placements (News Feed, Stories, Instagram, etc.).

How to Run an A/B Test?

1. **Create Two or More Variations**: Keep one element constant and change only one variable.

2. **Run the Test for a Sufficient Duration**: Allow at least 7-14 days for reliable results.

3. **Analyze the Data**: Compare performance metrics to identify the winning version.

4. **Implement the Best Version**: Use the best-performing ad and iterate further.

5. Conclusion: Making Data-Driven Decisions

Analyzing Facebook Ads performance is not just about looking at numbers—it's about extracting meaningful insights to refine and improve your campaigns. By focusing on key performance indicators, using Ads Manager effectively, and continuously optimizing your ads through testing, you can maximize the effectiveness of your Facebook Ads.

Key Takeaways:

✅ Focus on relevant KPIs such as CTR, CPC, conversions, and ROAS.

✅ Regularly review and adjust your targeting, creative, and budget.

✅ Use A/B testing to refine ad performance and improve engagement.

✅ Monitor ad fatigue and refresh your campaigns frequently.

By following these strategies, you can ensure that your Facebook Ads deliver better engagement, higher conversions, and a stronger return on investment (ROI).

CHAPTER VI
Managing Your Privacy and Security

7.1 Advanced Privacy Settings

7.1.1 Reviewing Your Privacy Checkup

Facebook provides a built-in **Privacy Checkup** tool that helps users review and adjust their privacy settings. This feature is essential for keeping your information secure and ensuring that you have control over who can see your content, personal details, and interactions. In this section, we will guide you through **how to access the Privacy Checkup tool, what settings it covers, and best practices for maintaining strong privacy on Facebook**.

1. What Is Facebook's Privacy Checkup?

The **Privacy Checkup** is a step-by-step tool designed to help users review and modify their privacy settings. It breaks privacy management into **five key areas**:

- **Who can see what you share**
- **How to keep your account secure**
- **How people can find you on Facebook**
- **Your data settings on Facebook**
- **Your ad preferences**

By going through these settings, you can **customize your privacy controls, limit exposure to strangers, and secure your account** against unauthorized access.

2. How to Access Facebook's Privacy Checkup

To access the **Privacy Checkup**, follow these steps:

1. Open Facebook and **log in to your account**.

2. Click on your **profile picture** at the top right corner (on desktop) or tap the **menu button (≡)** on mobile.

3. Select **"Settings & privacy"**, then choose **"Privacy Checkup"**.

4. Facebook will guide you through a series of **privacy settings grouped into different categories**.

Once inside the **Privacy Checkup tool**, you can start adjusting your settings to **protect your personal data and control who sees your content**.

---

3. Step-by-Step Guide to Privacy Checkup Categories

Now, let's go through **each section of the Privacy Checkup** and explain what settings you should adjust for better security and privacy.

3.1 Who Can See What You Share?

This section helps you **manage the visibility of your profile information, posts, and stories**.

a) Profile Information

Here, you can review who has access to your **phone number, email, birthday, and relationship status**. To adjust these:

- Click on each field (e.g., phone number) and choose one of the following visibility options:

  - **Public** (visible to everyone)

  - **Friends** (only your friends can see it)

  - **Only Me** (completely private)

  - **Custom** (you can choose specific people or lists)

- It's **highly recommended** to set sensitive information like **phone numbers and email addresses** to **"Only Me"** or at least "Friends."

b) Future Posts and Stories

- **Future posts**: This controls who will see your posts by default. Set this to **"Friends"** or "Only Me" instead of "Public" unless you want your content visible to everyone.

- **Stories**: You can limit who sees your Facebook Stories. Choose between **Public, Friends, or Custom Lists**.

c) Posts You've Shared in the Past

- If you have **old public posts** that you no longer want everyone to see, use the **"Limit Past Posts"** option. This will change all past posts from "Public" to "Friends Only" at once.

d) Blocking

- If there are people you do not want to **interact with** on Facebook, you can **block them**. Blocking prevents them from seeing your profile, posts, or messaging you.

3.2 How to Keep Your Account Secure

This section focuses on securing your **password, login settings, and two-factor authentication (2FA)**.

a) Reviewing Your Password Strength

- Use a strong password with **a mix of letters, numbers, and symbols**.

- Avoid using easily guessed passwords like **birthdays, pet names, or "123456"**.

- If your password is weak, change it immediately.

b) Enabling Two-Factor Authentication (2FA)

- This extra security step **requires a verification code in addition to your password** when logging in.

- To enable 2FA:

  1. Go to **Settings & privacy > Security and Login**.

2. Select **"Use two-factor authentication"** and follow the instructions.

3. Choose between a **text message (SMS)** or an **authentication app** (recommended).

c) Managing Login Alerts

- Facebook can notify you if someone logs into your account from an **unrecognized device**.

- To activate login alerts:

  o Go to **Settings & privacy > Security and Login**.

  o Click **"Get alerts about unrecognized logins"** and choose how you want to be notified (**via Facebook, email, or SMS**).

3.3 How People Can Find You on Facebook

This section helps you **control who can send friend requests and how people can search for you.**

a) Who Can Send You Friend Requests?

- Choose between **"Everyone"** (anyone can send requests) or **"Friends of Friends"** (recommended for more privacy).

b) Who Can Look You Up Using Your Phone Number or Email?

- Set this to **"Friends" or "Only Me"** to prevent strangers from finding your profile.

c) Do You Want Search Engines to Link to Your Facebook Profile?

- Disable this option to **prevent your Facebook profile from appearing in Google search results**.

3.4 Your Data Settings on Facebook

This section controls **which apps and websites have access to your Facebook data.**

a) Reviewing Connected Apps

- Check which **third-party apps and websites** are linked to your Facebook account.

- Remove any **apps you no longer use** to minimize data exposure.

b) Managing Facebook Activity Off-Site

- Facebook tracks your online activity on **other websites**.

- To limit this, go to **Settings > Your Facebook Information > Off-Facebook Activity** and **clear history**.

3.5 Your Ad Preferences

Facebook uses your data for personalized ads. You can **limit ad tracking and control what information advertisers can use**.

a) Reviewing Your Ad Interests

- Go to **Settings > Ads > Ad Preferences**.

- Remove topics that you don't want Facebook to use for ad targeting.

b) Turning Off Personalized Ads

- Under **"Ad Settings"**, set all options to **"Not Allowed"** to reduce targeted advertising.

---

4. Best Practices for Privacy on Facebook

To maintain **strong privacy protection**, follow these key tips:

- **Regularly review** your privacy settings using the Privacy Checkup tool.

- **Enable two-factor authentication** to protect against unauthorized access.

- **Limit the visibility** of sensitive personal information.

- **Be cautious with friend requests** from unknown people.

- **Review and remove old posts** that might contain personal information.

- **Check connected apps and services** and remove unnecessary ones.

- **Adjust ad settings** to limit data collection.

5. Final Thoughts

The **Privacy Checkup** is a crucial tool for keeping your Facebook account **secure and private**. By regularly reviewing and updating these settings, you can ensure that **your personal data remains protected while still enjoying Facebook's features**. Always stay vigilant and proactive in managing your online presence!

7.1.2 Controlling Tagging and Mentions

Facebook's tagging and mention features allow users to identify and reference other people in posts, comments, and photos. While these features can enhance social interaction, they also raise privacy concerns, as they can lead to unwanted exposure of personal information. Controlling how you are tagged and mentioned on Facebook is crucial for managing your online presence and ensuring that your privacy preferences are respected.

This section provides a step-by-step guide on how to manage tagging and mentions, including adjusting settings, reviewing tags before they appear, removing unwanted tags, and setting up restrictions to control who can tag or mention you.

1. Understanding Facebook's Tagging and Mention Features

What is Tagging?

Tagging on Facebook allows users to highlight or mention specific individuals in various types of content, including:

- **Posts and status updates** – Users can tag others by typing their name or using the "@" symbol.

- **Photos and videos** – Users can tag people in images and videos to indicate who is in them.

- **Comments** – Users can tag others in comment sections to get their attention.

- **Stories and reels** – Users can tag people in short-form content that disappears after 24 hours.

What is Mentioning?

Mentions work similarly to tagging, but they do not necessarily link directly to a person's profile in the same way. When someone mentions you in a post or comment using your name, you may receive a notification depending on your privacy settings.

The Risks of Uncontrolled Tagging and Mentions

While tagging and mentioning can be useful for engagement and social interaction, they also come with privacy risks, such as:

- **Exposure to unwanted audiences** – You may be tagged in posts that are public, making your profile visible to people outside your friend list.

- **Association with inappropriate or misleading content** – Others might tag you in posts or photos that you do not approve of.

- **Spam and phishing attempts** – Some users exploit tagging to spread scams or malicious content.

- **Over-tagging and unwanted notifications** – Frequent tagging can lead to excessive notifications and cluttered activity logs.

To prevent these issues, it is essential to configure your tagging and mention settings properly.

2. Adjusting Tagging and Mention Settings

Facebook provides several options to control how you are tagged and mentioned. To access these settings:

1. **Go to Facebook Settings**

   o   Click on your profile picture in the top right corner of Facebook.

   o   Select **Settings & privacy**, then click **Settings**.

2. **Navigate to the Privacy Settings**

   o   In the left-hand menu, select **Privacy**.

   o   Scroll down to the **Profile and Tagging** section.

3. **Manage Who Can Tag You**

- o Under **Tagging**, find the setting **Who can tag you in posts?**

- o Click **Edit** and choose from the following options:

  - **Everyone** – Anyone on Facebook can tag you.

  - **Friends of friends** – Only people who are mutual friends with your friends can tag you.

  - **Friends** – Only your direct friends can tag you.

  - **Only me** – No one can tag you except yourself.

4. **Control Post Visibility for Tags**

   - o Under **Reviewing**, enable **Review tags people add to your posts before the tags appear on Facebook.**

   - o This setting lets you approve or reject tags before they become visible.

5. **Restrict Who Sees Tagged Posts on Your Timeline**

   - o Under **Profile and Tagging**, find **Who can see posts you're tagged in on your profile?**

   - o Click **Edit** and choose from:

     - **Everyone** – Anyone on Facebook can see posts where you are tagged.

     - **Friends of friends** – Friends of the person who tagged you can also see the post.

     - **Friends** – Only your direct friends can see tagged posts.

     - **Only me** – No one except you can see posts you are tagged in.

6. **Control Mentions in Comments and Posts**

   - o Facebook does not allow users to disable mentions completely, but you can manage notifications and visibility.

   - o Under **Notifications settings**, turn off notifications for mentions if you do not want to be alerted when someone mentions you.

3. Reviewing and Removing Tags

How to Review Tags Before They Appear on Your Timeline

If you have enabled tag review, you can approve or reject tags by:

1. **Going to Activity Log**

   o Click on your profile picture and select **Activity log** from the dropdown menu.

   o Navigate to the **Review section** and select **Tags review**.

2. **Reviewing Pending Tags**

   o Click on a tagged post to view it.

   o Choose **Approve** if you are okay with the tag or **Decline** to prevent it from appearing on your timeline.

How to Remove Yourself from a Tagged Post

If you are tagged in a post you do not want to be associated with, follow these steps:

1. **Find the Post**

   o Go to your activity log or search for the post in your timeline.

2. **Click on the Three-Dot Menu**

   o In the upper-right corner of the post, click the three-dot menu.

3. **Select "Remove Tag"**

   o Confirm that you want to remove yourself from the tagged post.

   o The tag will disappear, but the post will still exist on the original poster's timeline.

---

4. Blocking Tagging from Specific Users

If someone consistently tags you in unwanted posts, you can take further action:

1. **Limit Interactions**

- o Go to **Privacy Settings > Blocking**.

- o Enter the name of the person you want to block.

- o Select **Block** to prevent them from tagging or mentioning you.

2. **Report Abusive Tagging**

- o If someone is tagging you in inappropriate or harmful content, click the three-dot menu on the post and select **Report Post**.

- o Follow the instructions to report the user.

5. Best Practices for Managing Tags and Mentions

- **Regularly review your tagged content** – Periodically check your activity log to ensure no unwanted tags appear.

- **Enable tag review for better control** – This prevents surprise tagging from showing up without your approval.

- **Communicate your preferences with friends** – Let your friends know your tagging boundaries to avoid misunderstandings.

- **Use Facebook's audience selector wisely** – Restrict tagged content to specific groups when necessary.

- **Stay vigilant against spam tags** – Do not click on suspicious tags or mentions that may lead to scams.

Conclusion

Facebook's tagging and mention features can be useful but also present privacy challenges. By adjusting your privacy settings, reviewing tags before they appear, removing unwanted tags, and blocking problematic users, you can maintain control over your online identity. Taking proactive steps to manage these features ensures a safer and more enjoyable Facebook experience.

By following the detailed steps and best practices outlined in this guide, you can confidently control how others tag and mention you, protecting both your privacy and reputation on the platform.

7.2 Protecting Your Data

7.2.1 Downloading a Copy of Your Data

In an era where digital privacy is increasingly important, Facebook provides users with the ability to download a copy of their data. This feature allows you to have a personal backup of all the content you've shared, including posts, photos, messages, and even interactions with other users. Whether you want to keep records for personal use, migrate data to another platform, or simply review what Facebook has collected about you, downloading your data is a useful and empowering step.

This section will guide you through the entire process of downloading your Facebook data, including what information you can retrieve, how to customize your download, and best practices for handling and storing your data securely.

Why Download Your Facebook Data?

There are several reasons why you might want to download your Facebook data:

- **Personal Backup:** Keeping a copy of your posts, messages, and media files ensures that you won't lose important memories or conversations.

- **Reviewing Data Collection:** Facebook collects a vast amount of data about your interactions. Downloading your archive allows you to see exactly what the platform knows about you.

- **Deleting or Deactivating Account:** If you plan to leave Facebook, having a copy of your data ensures that you can retain any important information before permanently removing your account.

- **Legal or Business Records:** If you use Facebook for business purposes, downloading data might be necessary for compliance, customer interactions, or marketing history.

What Data Can You Download?

Facebook allows you to download a wide range of data, including but not limited to:

1. Personal Information

- Your profile details (name, birthday, contact information, etc.)
- Account settings
- Security and login details

2. Your Activity on Facebook

- Posts and comments
- Photos and videos uploaded by you
- Stories and Reels
- Messages and chats in Messenger
- Likes and reactions
- Groups you have joined
- Events you have attended or created

3. Friends and Connections

- Your friend list
- People you follow and who follow you
- Friend requests sent and received

4. Advertisements and Interactions

- Ads you have interacted with
- Advertisers who have your contact information
- Search history
- Location history (if enabled)

5. App and Device Information

- Devices used to access Facebook
- Login history and IP addresses

You can customize which of these data types to include in your download, as well as choose a specific date range or download everything from your account's history.

Step-by-Step Guide to Downloading Your Facebook Data

Step 1: Access the Facebook Settings Page

1. Log in to your Facebook account on a web browser.
2. Click on your profile picture in the top right corner.
3. Select **"Settings & Privacy"** from the dropdown menu.
4. Click **"Settings"** to open the main settings page.

Step 2: Navigate to the Data Download Section

1. In the left-hand menu, click on **"Your Facebook Information"**.
2. Look for the option labeled **"Download Your Information"** and click on it.

Step 3: Select the Data You Want to Download

1. You will see a list of all the types of data available for download.
2. Use the checkboxes to select specific categories, or click **"Deselect All"** and choose only the ones you need.
3. You can filter the data by date range or download everything from the time your account was created.
4. Choose the **file format**:
   - **HTML** (easier to view with a browser)
   - **JSON** (better for importing data into other platforms)

5. Select the **media quality** for photos and videos (high, medium, or low).

Step 4: Request the Download

1. Click the **"Create File"** button.

2. Facebook will start processing your request, which may take from a few minutes to several hours, depending on the amount of data.

Step 5: Download Your Data

1. Once your file is ready, you will receive a **notification** from Facebook.

2. Return to the **"Download Your Information"** section.

3. Click **"Available Files"** and then **"Download"** next to your file.

4. Enter your **password** for security verification.

5. The file will be downloaded as a **.zip archive** to your device.

How to Open and Explore Your Downloaded Data

Extracting the ZIP File

- Locate the downloaded **.zip file** in your computer's **Downloads** folder.

- Right-click the file and select **"Extract"** or use an archive tool like **WinRAR** or **7-Zip**.

Exploring the Data

- If you chose **HTML format**, open the **index.html** file in a web browser. This will present your data in an easy-to-navigate format.

- If you chose **JSON format**, you may need a text editor or a data viewer like **Notepad++** or **Visual Studio Code** to properly view the files.

Best Practices for Handling Your Facebook Data

1. Store Your Data Securely

- Because this file contains sensitive personal information, store it in a **secure location**, such as an encrypted external hard drive or a password-protected cloud service.

- Avoid storing it on **public or shared devices**.

2. Do Not Share Your Data File

- Your downloaded file includes private messages, personal details, and possibly location history. Do not upload it to third-party services unless necessary.

3. Delete Unneeded Copies

- If you no longer need the downloaded data, **permanently delete** the file rather than leaving it exposed on your device.

Troubleshooting Common Issues

1. My Download is Taking Too Long

- Large accounts with years of data may take several hours to process.

- If the request is stuck, try **canceling** and submitting a new request.

2. The Download Link Expired

- Facebook provides a **limited time** to download your data. If your link expired, you need to request a new file.

3. I Can't Find My File After Downloading

- Check your **Downloads** folder.

- If you can't locate it, try searching for **Facebook-data.zip** in your file explorer.

Conclusion

Downloading your Facebook data is an essential step in maintaining control over your online presence. Whether you're backing up personal memories, reviewing privacy settings, or preparing to delete your account, having a copy of your information gives you greater flexibility and security.

By following the steps outlined in this guide, you can efficiently download, explore, and manage your Facebook data while ensuring it remains safe and secure. In the next section, we'll discuss how to **deactivate or permanently delete your Facebook account**, including the key differences between both options and what happens to your data after deletion.

7.2.2 Deactivating or Deleting Your Account

In today's digital world, social media accounts such as Facebook store vast amounts of personal information, making it essential to understand the options available to manage your account's privacy. Facebook offers two options for managing your account when you decide you no longer want to use the platform — **deactivating** your account or **deleting** it entirely. Each choice has different consequences, and it is important to understand them fully before making a decision.

In this section, we will guide you through the process of deactivating or deleting your Facebook account, explain the differences between the two, and help you choose the option best suited for your needs.

What is the Difference Between Deactivating and Deleting Your Account?

Before diving into the steps for deactivating or deleting your Facebook account, it's important to understand the difference between the two options:

1. **Deactivating Your Account:**

    o **Temporary Suspension**: Deactivating your account means temporarily suspending your Facebook presence. It's an option if you want to take a break from Facebook without permanently losing all of your data.

    o **Data Retention**: When you deactivate your account, Facebook retains all of your information, such as your profile, photos, posts, and messages, but it will be hidden from others. This allows you to reactivate your account at any time without losing your data.

- o **Reactivation**: You can reactivate your account by simply logging back in. Your friends can still see messages you've sent them in the past, but your timeline and other activity will remain hidden while your account is deactivated.

2. **Deleting Your Account:**

   - o **Permanent Removal**: Deleting your account is a permanent decision. Once you delete your Facebook account, you will lose access to all of your posts, messages, and data stored on the platform.

   - o **Data Deletion**: Facebook claims that most of your data will be erased from their servers within a few days of deletion, although some backup copies may remain for a longer period.

   - o **Irreversible**: Deletion is irreversible. Once your account is deleted, you will not be able to recover any of the information associated with it. If you want to use Facebook again in the future, you would need to create a new account.

Now that we've established the difference, let's explore the steps for both deactivating and deleting your Facebook account in detail.

Deactivating Your Facebook Account

If you want to take a break from Facebook without permanently losing your information, deactivating your account is the way to go. Here's how to deactivate your account:

Step 1: Accessing Your Facebook Settings

1. **Log into Facebook**: First, log into your Facebook account by entering your username and password at www.facebook.com.

2. **Go to Settings**: In the top-right corner of your Facebook page, click on the small downward arrow (also called the "dropdown menu") next to your profile picture. From the dropdown menu, select **Settings & Privacy** and then **Settings**.

Step 2: Navigating to the "Your Facebook Information" Section

1. **Select Your Facebook Information**: On the left sidebar of your settings page, look for the section labeled **Your Facebook Information**. Click on it to access more options.

2. **Choose Deactivation and Deletion**: Under this section, you will see an option called **Deactivation and Deletion**. Click on this option to proceed.

Step 3: Deactivating Your Account

1. **Select Deactivate Account**: You will be presented with two options: **Deactivate Account** or **Delete Account**. Since you are opting to deactivate your account, choose **Deactivate Account**.

2. **Confirm Your Decision**: Facebook will ask you to confirm your decision to deactivate. You'll need to enter your password again to proceed.

3. **Optional: Provide a Reason for Deactivation**: Facebook will ask why you are deactivating your account. You can choose from a list of reasons or skip this step if you prefer.

4. **Choose to Stay Connected**: Facebook will offer you the option to receive email notifications, even though your account is deactivated. You can choose to leave this unchecked if you wish to stop all communications.

5. **Click "Deactivate"**: Once you've made your selections, click the **Deactivate** button. Your account will now be deactivated.

Your Facebook account will be hidden from others, but your data will remain intact. You can reactivate your account at any time by simply logging back into Facebook with your username and password.

Deleting Your Facebook Account

If you are certain you want to permanently erase your Facebook presence, deleting your account is the final step. Here's how to delete your account:

Step 1: Accessing Your Facebook Settings

1. **Log into Facebook**: As with deactivation, begin by logging into your Facebook account.

2. **Go to Settings**: Click on the downward arrow in the top-right corner of your Facebook page. Then, go to **Settings & Privacy** and click on **Settings**.

Step 2: Navigating to "Deactivation and Deletion"

1. **Your Facebook Information**: From the left sidebar, select **Your Facebook Information**.

2. **Deactivation and Deletion**: Click on the **Deactivation and Deletion** option.

Step 3: Selecting Account Deletion

1. **Choose Delete Account**: On the page where you're asked to select between deactivation and deletion, choose **Delete Account**. This will begin the permanent deletion process.

2. **Confirm Your Decision**: Facebook will warn you that deleting your account is permanent and irreversible. You will lose access to all data, such as messages, photos, and posts.

3. **Enter Your Password**: To confirm your decision, you will be asked to enter your password.

4. **Click "Delete Account"**: Once you've confirmed your password and acknowledged the consequences of deletion, click **Delete Account**.

Your account is now scheduled for deletion. Facebook will keep your account active for 30 days, during which time you can still cancel the deletion request by logging back in. After the 30-day period, your account and all associated data will be permanently deleted.

What Happens After Deletion?

Once your account is permanently deleted:

- **Loss of Data**: You will lose access to all of your posts, messages, photos, and any data you've shared or stored on Facebook.

- **Irreversible**: After 30 days, your account will be gone forever. If you decide to return to Facebook, you will need to create a new account from scratch.

- **Third-Party Apps**: If you used your Facebook account to log into other apps or websites (such as games, email services, or subscription services), you may lose access to these services unless you update your login information beforehand.

When Should You Deactivate vs. Delete?

Choosing between deactivating or deleting your account depends on your needs:

- **Deactivate**: Choose to deactivate if you need a break from Facebook but want to retain the option to return later. This is a good option if you're unsure about leaving the platform permanently.

- **Delete**: Choose to delete if you're certain that you want to remove your presence from Facebook entirely and are ready to say goodbye to your data on the platform.

It's important to consider that Facebook will retain some information even after you delete your account, such as data in backup servers or any messages you've sent to others. If complete privacy is your goal, you may want to ensure that all linked apps and data are properly managed before deletion.

Conclusion

Deactivating or deleting your Facebook account is a big decision that should be made after careful consideration. If you simply want a break from Facebook, deactivation is a convenient and reversible option. However, if you've decided to part ways with Facebook permanently, deletion is the path you should take. Remember to back up any important information, such as photos and messages, before proceeding with either option.

By following the steps outlined in this guide, you can ensure that your decision regarding your Facebook account is well-informed, secure, and aligns with your privacy preferences.

7.3 Avoiding Online Threats

7.3.1 Identifying Fake Profiles

In today's digital world, Facebook is not only a platform for connecting with friends and family but also a place where individuals can encounter various types of online threats, including fake profiles. These profiles are created by malicious individuals who may have harmful intentions, such as spreading misinformation, committing fraud, or attempting to manipulate others. This section will help you understand how to identify fake profiles, what red flags to look for, and how to protect yourself from potential harm.

Why Fake Profiles Are a Concern

Fake profiles can be dangerous in several ways:

- **Scams and Fraud**: Fake profiles are often used to scam individuals. For example, they may be used to create fake fundraising campaigns, offering fake job opportunities, or even pretending to be someone you know in order to ask for money.

- **Phishing Attacks**: Fake profiles can attempt to trick you into sharing personal information such as passwords, credit card numbers, or even bank account details by posing as legitimate entities or people.

- **Social Engineering**: Scammers may use fake profiles to manipulate or influence you emotionally, often leading to compromised trust or decisions.

- **Misinformation**: Fake accounts might spread false information or conspiracy theories, often designed to influence public opinion or manipulate emotions.

- **Cyberbullying and Harassment**: Fake profiles can be used to harass, intimidate, or bully individuals without facing accountability, as these profiles are often hard to trace.

Knowing how to spot these fraudulent accounts is essential in protecting your online security and privacy. Let's dive into the most effective ways to identify fake Facebook profiles.

How to Identify Fake Profiles

1. Unrealistic Profile Picture

A profile picture is often the first impression of a Facebook user. Fake accounts frequently use stock images, photos of celebrities, or images stolen from other people's social media pages. These pictures are sometimes too polished or generic to seem real.

- **How to Spot It**: You can use a reverse image search tool like Google Images to see if the profile picture appears elsewhere on the internet. If the image is frequently used across multiple accounts or websites, it's likely fake.

- **Additional Tip**: Fake profiles sometimes use photos that are not of the user's own identity. These photos can be overly professional, glamourized, or just suspiciously perfect.

2. Limited Personal Information

Real Facebook users typically have rich, detailed profiles with personal information, hobbies, work history, education, and mutual connections. Fake profiles, on the other hand, are often sparse and lack such information. If the account does not have meaningful details like a bio, location, or friends, it could be a red flag.

- **How to Spot It**: Check the "About" section of the profile. A lack of a proper introduction, vague or inconsistent information, and missing family or work history should raise concerns.

- **Additional Tip**: Fake profiles may also have very few or no posts. Social media accounts typically feature photos and updates from the user's life, whereas fake profiles may not have any meaningful posts or interactions.

3. Unrealistic Name or Username

Many fake accounts use overly simplistic names such as "John Doe" or "Jane Smith," or strange combinations of letters and numbers that seem computer-generated. Additionally, fake accounts sometimes use names that are culturally out of place or odd combinations of common first and last names.

- **How to Spot It**: If the name seems too generic, or if the profile lacks a recognizable name, it might be fake. Fake profiles may also use fake names to conceal their real identities.

- **Additional Tip**: If the account's username has numbers or symbols that seem unnatural, especially when they don't match the user's name in the profile, it could indicate a fake profile.

4. Newly Created Account with No Friends or Mutual Friends

A common feature of fake profiles is that they don't have many friends, or they have none at all. These profiles may also lack mutual friends who can vouch for their authenticity. In contrast, real Facebook accounts typically have several mutual connections with you, especially if you share the same networks, interests, or community.

- **How to Spot It**: Look at the friend count and mutual friends. If you find a profile with very few friends or zero mutual friends with you or your connections, proceed with caution.

- **Additional Tip**: Fake accounts often try to add people who have little or no mutual connections, hoping they can get away with connecting with strangers.

5. Inconsistent or Generic Posts

Fake profiles rarely post original content, and when they do, the content is often generic, vague, or irrelevant. Fake accounts may post fake inspirational quotes, spammy messages, or attempt to get likes through clickbait tactics. Real profiles usually have a combination of posts about personal experiences, thoughts, interests, and interactions with friends or family.

- **How to Spot It**: Check the posts made by the profile. If they mostly consist of repetitive content, links to dubious websites, or generic memes, this is a major indicator that the account is fake.

- **Additional Tip**: Fake accounts may also share political or controversial posts that seem designed to provoke emotional reactions. Look for posts that don't match the tone of a typical Facebook user's content.

6. Strange or Suspicious Behavior

One of the most telling signs of a fake profile is unusual or suspicious behavior, such as sending unsolicited friend requests, private messages, or asking for money or other personal favors. Fake accounts often try to build rapport quickly and then ask for personal information, gifts, or financial support.

- **How to Spot It**: If you receive a message from someone you've never met asking for personal favors, money, or suspicious links, proceed with extreme caution.

- **Additional Tip**: Fake accounts may also follow an aggressive approach, such as rapidly sending friend requests or attempting to message multiple people in a short period.

7. Profile Activity Does Not Match the Profile Picture

Sometimes, fake accounts might post activity that doesn't correlate with the image they present. For instance, if the profile picture shows someone who appears young and professional, but the posts or messages reflect interests or behavior more typical of an older or different demographic, this can be a clear warning sign.

- **How to Spot It**: Compare the profile's behavior with its image. Fake profiles may seem to have contradictory interests, hobbies, or activities that don't align with the person they're pretending to be.

- **Additional Tip**: Fake profiles are often too eager to connect, offering generic messages like "I saw your profile, and you look amazing" to get attention. If the messages seem forced or unnatural, they could be a scam.

8. Checking the Profile's Activity History

One of the most reliable ways to identify a fake profile is to analyze the account's activity history. Authentic Facebook profiles typically have a history of engagement with friends, groups, pages, and posts over a period of time. Fake profiles, on the other hand, tend to have little or no history of interactions, particularly in the way of meaningful posts or engagement with other users.

- **How to Spot It**: Look for engagement. If the account has been active for a long time but doesn't have much content or interaction, or if all interactions are new and span a short amount of time, it could be fake.

- **Additional Tip**: Check for the date when the account was created. Fake profiles are often newly created and don't have an established history.

What to Do if You Suspect a Fake Profile

If you come across a profile that you suspect is fake, there are a few actions you can take:

- **Report the Profile**: Facebook allows you to report suspicious profiles. You can do this by clicking on the three dots next to the profile and selecting "Find support or report profile."

- **Block the Profile**: If you don't want to engage with the suspicious profile further, you can block the account. This will prevent the person from sending you friend requests, messages, or seeing your content.

- **Avoid Sharing Personal Information**: Never share sensitive data with individuals on Facebook, especially if you're unsure of their identity. This includes your home address, phone number, credit card details, and bank account information.

- **Educate Others**: If you find a fake profile that may be trying to scam others, alert your friends or anyone who may be at risk of falling for it.

Conclusion

Identifying fake profiles is an important part of maintaining a secure and positive online experience. By recognizing the common signs of a fraudulent account, you can protect yourself and your Facebook network from potential threats. Always be cautious when interacting with profiles that seem suspicious, and trust your instincts if something feels off.

7.3.2 Reporting Suspicious Activity

In today's digital age, online threats are a prevalent concern, and social media platforms like Facebook are often targeted by malicious actors seeking to exploit users. Facebook has a built-in system that allows users to report suspicious activity and potential threats. Knowing how to report suspicious activity is essential to keeping both your account and others safe. In this section, we'll walk through the process of identifying suspicious behavior and provide a detailed guide on how to report it effectively to Facebook.

What is Suspicious Activity on Facebook?

Before we dive into how to report suspicious activity, it's important to first understand what counts as suspicious activity on Facebook. Suspicious behavior can manifest in various forms, and it's crucial to recognize these signs so that you can take appropriate action quickly. Here are some common examples of suspicious activity:

1. **Phishing Scams**: These are fraudulent attempts to steal your personal information, such as login credentials, by posing as a trusted source (such as Facebook itself, or other known organizations).

2. **Fake Profiles**: Sometimes, people create fake accounts to impersonate others or to engage in scams or harassment. This can include profiles pretending to be you or someone you know.

3. **Malicious Links or Attachments**: Posts or messages with links that seem out of place or lead to websites that you don't recognize can often be attempts to trick you into downloading malware or giving away sensitive information.

4. **Harassment and Threats**: Online harassment, bullying, and threats are not only upsetting but can also indicate malicious intent, such as intimidation or coercion.

5. **Spam or Unwanted Content**: Accounts posting irrelevant, repetitive, or promotional content in an attempt to manipulate or exploit others fall under suspicious activity.

Why Should You Report Suspicious Activity?

Reporting suspicious activity is a critical part of maintaining a safe online community. Here's why reporting is so important:

1. **Protect Your Privacy and Data**: Reporting threats ensures that your personal information and data remain protected from malicious attempts to steal or misuse them.

2. **Prevent Scams from Spreading**: The faster suspicious behavior is reported, the less likely it is that others will fall victim to scams or phishing attacks.

3. **Protect Others**: By reporting suspicious accounts or activity, you help protect not just yourself, but also your friends, family, and broader network.

4. **Improve Facebook's Security**: Every report made contributes to Facebook's efforts to improve its security systems. The more reports they receive, the better their detection systems become.

How to Identify Suspicious Activity

Knowing what to look out for is the first step toward identifying suspicious activity. Here are some signs to watch for:

1. **Unexpected Messages**: If someone you don't know is sending you messages with links or attachments that seem irrelevant or out of place, it could be a scam or phishing attempt.

2. **Unusual Friend Requests**: If you receive a friend request from a person or account you do not recognize, especially if the profile seems incomplete, it could be a fake profile.

3. **Inappropriate Content**: If you notice posts that are explicit, harassing, or seem like spam on your timeline or in groups you belong to, this could be a sign of suspicious activity.

4. **Strange Account Behavior**: If you notice that your account is being used in ways you didn't authorize, such as messages being sent from your account without your knowledge, it could mean that your account is compromised.

5. **Impersonation**: If you notice someone creating an account in your name or the name of someone you know, that's a clear red flag for potential malicious intent.

How to Report Suspicious Activity on Facebook

Facebook has a robust system for reporting suspicious activity, and it's important to use it whenever you encounter something suspicious. Here's how to report suspicious activity in different cases:

1. Reporting Suspicious Messages

If you receive a message that seems suspicious or contains harmful links, here's what to do:

1. **Open the Message**: First, go to the message in question.

2. **Click on the Three Dots**: In the top right corner of the message, you'll see three horizontal dots. Click on them.

3. **Select "Report"**: From the options that appear, click on "Report." Facebook will ask you to specify the nature of the message, so choose "Spam" or "Harassment" depending on the context.

4. **Follow the Prompts**: You'll be asked to provide more information if necessary, such as why you think the message is suspicious. Once you've completed the steps, submit the report.

Important Tip: Always be cautious about clicking on links in messages from unfamiliar senders. Even if the link seems legitimate, it's better to report the message and avoid clicking.

2. Reporting Fake or Impersonated Profiles

If you come across an account that you believe is fake or impersonating someone, you can easily report it:

1. **Go to the Profile**: Navigate to the person's profile page.

2. **Click on the Three Dots**: In the bottom right corner of the profile cover photo, you'll see three dots. Click them to open the options.

3. **Select "Find Support or Report Profile"**: A menu will appear asking you to select the issue. Choose "Fake Account" or "Impersonation" based on what applies.

4. **Follow the Prompts**: Facebook may ask for additional details, such as the reason for your report or if you believe the account is pretending to be someone else. Complete these fields to submit your report.

Important Tip: If the fake account is impersonating someone you know, you should also inform that person so they can report it as well.

---

3. Reporting Suspicious Posts or Content

If you see suspicious or inappropriate posts, follow these steps to report them:

1. **Click on the Three Dots**: On the top right corner of the post, click the three dots.

2. **Select "Report Post"**: From the options, click "Report Post."

3. **Choose a Reason**: Facebook will ask why you are reporting the post. Options could include "It's offensive," "It's spam," or "It's a scam."

4. **Follow the Prompts**: You may be asked for more details, such as explaining why the post is harmful. Provide the necessary information and submit the report.

Important Tip: If the content is inappropriate or violates Facebook's community standards, don't hesitate to report it immediately.

---

4. Reporting Suspicious Ads

If you come across an ad that seems misleading or suspicious, it's essential to report it:

1. **Click on the Three Dots**: On the top right corner of the ad, click the three dots.

2. **Select "Report Ad"**: From the dropdown menu, choose "Report Ad."

3. **Choose a Reason**: Facebook will ask you to select why you think the ad is suspicious. Options include misleading content, deceptive tactics, or it being irrelevant.

4. **Submit the Report**: Follow the prompts to finalize and submit your report.

Important Tip: If an ad seems too good to be true (for example, offering things for free or at suspiciously low prices), report it right away.

What Happens After You Report Suspicious Activity?

After you submit a report, Facebook will review the issue to determine whether it violates their Community Standards. If the reported content, profile, or message is deemed suspicious or harmful, Facebook may take several actions:

- **Remove the Content**: Facebook may remove posts, profiles, or ads that violate their standards.

- **Warn the User**: In some cases, the account involved may receive a warning.

- **Block or Ban the User**: In more severe cases, Facebook may block the account or ban the user from the platform.

While Facebook doesn't always provide specific details about the action taken, they do take reports seriously and work to prevent suspicious activity from spreading.

Conclusion: Stay Vigilant and Report Suspicious Activity

Reporting suspicious activity is crucial for maintaining a safe and enjoyable experience on Facebook. By recognizing the signs of scams, impersonation, phishing attempts, and harassment, you can protect yourself and others from potential threats. Remember, Facebook's security team relies on user reports to help maintain a safe environment, so don't hesitate to report any suspicious activity you encounter.

By using Facebook's built-in reporting tools and remaining vigilant about your privacy and security, you contribute to the broader effort to ensure that the platform remains a trusted space for everyone.

CHAPTER VII
Advanced Facebook Tips and Tricks

8.1 Optimizing Your Profile for Networking

In the world of social media, your profile is your personal brand. It is often the first impression people get of you online, whether they are a potential employer, business partner, or someone you meet through mutual interests. When it comes to Facebook, optimizing your profile for networking is key to making meaningful connections and creating opportunities for personal and professional growth. This section will guide you through the essential steps to ensure your Facebook profile is primed for networking success.

1. Choose the Right Profile Picture

Your profile picture is the first thing people notice when they visit your page, so it's essential to choose a photo that is both professional and approachable. Here are a few tips for selecting the best profile picture for networking:

- **Professional Look:** Choose a clear, high-quality image where you look confident and approachable. For professional networking, a headshot with a neutral background is ideal. Avoid casual or overly playful pictures, as they might not convey the right message.

- **Appropriate Attire:** If your goal is to network for business or career-related reasons, it's essential to dress appropriately. Depending on your profession, this could mean wearing business attire or simply something clean and neat.

- **Smile and Make Eye Contact:** A friendly smile and direct eye contact convey confidence and warmth, making people more likely to engage with you.

- **Avoid Group Photos:** While group photos with friends or colleagues are fun, they may confuse visitors about who you are. Choose a picture where you are the sole focus.

Once you've uploaded your profile picture, ensure it's visible to everyone or at least to people you want to connect with.

2. Craft an Engaging and Professional Cover Photo

Your cover photo, the large banner image at the top of your profile, is another opportunity to showcase your personal brand. Unlike the profile picture, your cover photo gives you more space to get creative. Here's how to optimize it:

- **Reflect Your Interests or Profession:** Use a cover photo that aligns with your career, business, or interests. For instance, if you work in graphic design, you could use a cover photo of your portfolio. If you're passionate about travel, use an image that highlights your adventures.

- **Keep it Clean and Simple:** Avoid cluttered or overly busy images. Instead, opt for a clean and professional image that speaks to who you are. This can be an inspiring quote, a logo, or a simple photo related to your field.

- **Match Your Profile Picture Style:** For consistency, choose a cover photo that complements your profile picture in tone. A mismatch between your profile and cover photos can make your page look disjointed.

3. Write a Compelling and Concise Bio

Your bio is an essential element of your Facebook profile, especially when networking. It gives visitors a snapshot of who you are, your skills, and your interests. To optimize your bio for networking, follow these steps:

- **Be Clear and Concise:** Write a short, professional bio that introduces yourself in a few sentences. State your profession or area of expertise and mention any relevant achievements or goals. Keep it focused on what is most important for the audience you want to attract.

- **Use Keywords:** Think about the types of people you want to connect with on Facebook and use keywords in your bio that will resonate with them. If you're a marketing professional, include terms like "digital marketing," "content strategy," or "SEO" to ensure people in your field can find you.

- **Add a Personal Touch:** While it's important to keep things professional, don't be afraid to share a little about your personality. Mention hobbies, passions, or causes you care about. This can help others feel more connected to you on a personal level.

- **Call to Action:** If you're open to collaborations, job offers, or networking opportunities, include a call to action. A simple line like "Feel free to connect with me if you're interested in digital marketing or tech!" can invite meaningful engagement.

4. Customize Your Facebook URL

Facebook allows you to create a custom URL for your profile, making it easier for people to find you and remember your profile. This is particularly important for networking because you'll often share your profile link with others. To customize your URL:

1. Go to your Facebook profile page.

2. Click on the "Edit Profile" button.

3. Under the "General" tab, look for the option to "Edit Username."

4. Choose a username that reflects your name or your professional brand. Keep it short and easy to remember.

By having a clean, professional URL, you make it easier for people to find you, and your profile looks more polished.

5. Share Valuable and Relevant Content

One of the best ways to optimize your profile for networking is by sharing content that adds value to others. By posting relevant and insightful content, you not only demonstrate your expertise but also engage with your audience in a meaningful way. Here's how to do it:

- **Post Regularly:** To stay top of mind, post content consistently. Whether it's industry news, inspirational quotes, or updates on your professional achievements, regular posting keeps your profile active and visible to your connections.

- **Share Your Insights and Knowledge:** Facebook is a great platform to share what you know. If you're an expert in your field, use your posts to provide value by sharing tips, insights, or advice. This helps establish you as a thought leader.

- **Engage with Comments:** When you post content, be sure to interact with comments and messages. Responding to people's feedback builds relationships and shows that you're approachable and willing to engage.

- **Curate Third-Party Content:** You don't always have to create content yourself. Sharing articles, blogs, or videos from others in your industry can position you as a well-rounded professional who stays up-to-date with trends and news.

6. Manage Your Friend List for Networking

Having a wide network on Facebook can be incredibly beneficial, but only if you manage it effectively. Here's how to maintain a network that will be valuable for your personal and professional growth:

- **Build a Diverse Network:** While it's tempting to add only people you know personally, Facebook's power lies in the ability to connect with people across industries and backgrounds. Reach out to professionals in your field, join relevant groups, and participate in conversations that align with your career or interests.

- **Organize Your Friends List:** Facebook allows you to categorize your friends into lists. Create specific lists for different types of connections—work colleagues, business contacts, family, friends, etc. This will help you filter what content each group sees and allow you to target your networking efforts more effectively.

- **Be Selective About Accepting Friend Requests:** While it's great to grow your network, be strategic about who you accept as a friend. Ensure they align with your networking goals. If you're building a professional network, you might want to limit your friend list to people with similar career interests or values.

- **Use the 'Follow' Feature:** If you're hesitant about accepting someone's friend request but still want to stay connected, use Facebook's "Follow" feature. By following someone, you can see their posts without being added as a friend. This is especially useful for professional networking.

7. Use Facebook Groups for Networking

Facebook Groups are a powerful tool for building relationships with like-minded professionals. Here's how to use them effectively:

- **Join Relevant Groups:** Find Facebook groups that align with your industry, career goals, or personal interests. Participate in discussions and contribute to the group by sharing valuable content or offering advice.

- **Create Your Own Group:** If you have a specific niche or area of expertise, consider creating your own Facebook group. This allows you to build a community around your personal brand and position yourself as a leader in your field.

- **Engage Actively in Groups:** Networking in groups is all about engagement. Comment on posts, share resources, and help others when you can. Networking isn't just about making connections—it's about building trust and offering value.

Optimizing your Facebook profile for networking isn't a one-time task; it's an ongoing process. By continuously updating your profile, sharing valuable content, and engaging with your connections, you can create a thriving online network that opens up new opportunities for both personal and professional growth.

8.2 Using Facebook Search Like a Pro

Facebook's search feature is one of its most powerful tools, but many users are unaware of its full potential. The search bar on Facebook does more than just help you find people and pages. It can be a gateway to discovering content, groups, events, and even targeted ads. This section will guide you through how to leverage Facebook's search functionality to enhance your user experience, find what you need faster, and uncover hidden gems on the platform.

Understanding the Facebook Search Bar

The Facebook search bar is located at the top of the Facebook interface, whether you're using the desktop or mobile version. By default, when you type into the search bar, Facebook offers suggestions like people, pages, posts, photos, videos, and more based on your interests and interactions. However, this is just the surface.

In the following sections, we'll break down how to effectively use Facebook's search bar to unlock deeper layers of the platform.

1. Search Filters: Narrowing Down Results

Facebook's search bar provides a range of filters to help you refine your search results. Here are the most common ways to use these filters:

People and Friends

- **Finding Specific People**: If you are searching for a specific person, simply type their name in the search bar. Facebook will show you a list of people who match that name. If the person you're looking for has a common name, you can refine your search by adding more keywords (e.g., their location, workplace, or mutual friends).

- **Mutual Friends**: Facebook's search algorithm prioritizes results based on mutual connections. So, if you're looking for someone, Facebook will list people you have mutual friends with near the top of the search results.

- **Searching for People by Interests**: If you want to find people with certain interests, such as a sport, hobby, or professional focus, you can search for groups, pages, or posts related to that interest. People involved in those topics are likely to appear in your results.

Pages and Public Figures

- **Business Pages**: Facebook's search is great for finding business pages, whether you're looking for a restaurant, clothing store, or software company. Simply type the name of the business or service you are looking for into the search bar.

- **Public Figures**: If you're looking for celebrities, politicians, or industry leaders, Facebook allows you to search for their official pages. When you search for someone famous, be mindful of fake or fan pages, as Facebook may suggest unofficial profiles as well.

Groups and Communities

- **Join and Explore Groups**: Facebook groups are a fantastic way to connect with like-minded people. You can search for groups based on topics you are passionate about, whether it's a professional industry, hobbies, or local community interests.

- **Advanced Group Search**: Facebook has made it easier to find relevant groups by providing search filters such as "Public" or "Private," "Closed," and group size. This helps you discover both large communities and more intimate, niche groups. If you're looking for specific topics like "marketing," "traveling," or "startups," you can add those terms to the search query.

Events

- **Finding Local and Virtual Events**: Facebook is a powerful tool for event discovery. If you want to attend a local event, you can use the search bar to find everything from concerts, art shows, networking events, and workshops happening near you. Facebook also allows you to search for online events such as webinars and virtual meetups.

- **Event Suggestions Based on Interests**: Facebook will tailor event recommendations based on your interests, past interactions, and location settings. If you frequently engage with a particular type of event, Facebook's search algorithm will prioritize those events in your feed.

2. Using Keywords and Hashtags Effectively

A great way to refine your Facebook search is by using specific keywords or hashtags. Hashtags make it easier to find posts, trends, and content related to particular topics. You can search for hashtags to explore discussions or follow trending topics.

Using Keywords

- **Keyword Precision**: To search for specific content, posts, or people, try using more precise keywords. For instance, if you're looking for marketing tips, type "digital marketing tips" into the search bar. Adding more specific terms will refine your results.

- **Refining Search for Posts**: If you want to find posts that are relevant to your search, use specific keywords like "#socialmedia" or "#AI." Posts with those hashtags or keywords will appear in the search results.

Hashtags

- **Hashtag Discovery**: Facebook has adopted hashtags from platforms like Instagram and Twitter, allowing users to discover posts around specific topics or trends. Simply search for a hashtag, and Facebook will show all public posts that have used that hashtag. This is particularly useful for keeping up with trends, events, or popular discussions.

- **Tracking Hashtags**: Facebook will show you hashtags related to your search query. This feature makes it easier to track what's trending, join in discussions, or follow your favorite topics.

3. Search for Specific Types of Content

Facebook offers several content-specific searches, allowing you to filter your search results based on the type of media you are looking for.

Searching for Photos and Videos

- **Searching for Photos**: To find images that are related to a specific keyword or event, use the "Photos" filter. This will help you search for images related to people, places, or things that are shared on Facebook.

- **Searching for Videos**: Videos are an essential part of Facebook, with millions being uploaded daily. You can search for videos using keywords like "recipe videos," "product reviews," or "vlogs," and filter your results by most recent or most popular.

- **Live Video Search**: Facebook allows you to search specifically for live videos. If you want to watch real-time content, you can search for live broadcasts on events, news, or entertainment.

Searching for Comments and Posts

- **Post-Specific Searches**: Facebook's search functionality allows you to find posts that include a specific keyword or phrase. To find comments that mention a particular topic, search for posts using relevant keywords.

- **Looking for Conversations**: Searching for specific words within Facebook's posts and comments lets you track conversations around certain news events, trending hashtags, or popular discussions.

---

4. Using Facebook Search with Advanced Operators

If you want to take your search capabilities even further, you can use advanced search operators on Facebook. These operators let you fine-tune your searches and get even more specific results.

Using Quotation Marks for Exact Matches

- When you use quotation marks around a phrase, Facebook will search for the exact phrase. For example, searching for "climate change discussion" will return posts, pages, and groups that include that exact phrase, rather than just posts that contain any of the words individually.

Boolean Search Operators

- **AND, OR, NOT**: These operators are useful if you want to combine or exclude specific words. For instance:

    o "travel AND blogging" will return posts that include both keywords.

    o "fitness OR health" will return posts with either of the keywords.

    o "marketing NOT ads" will exclude any posts with the word "ads."

5. Exploring Facebook's Saved Feature

Facebook offers the option to save content you come across during your search, which is an excellent way to track interesting posts, pages, events, and videos for later viewing.

Saving Posts and Content

- **Saving Individual Posts**: When you find a post you want to revisit later, click the three dots in the top right of the post and select "Save Post." It will be stored in your "Saved" section, accessible from your profile.

- **Saving Links, Videos, and More**: You can also save links, videos, events, and pages. This feature is great for users who want to keep track of content that resonates with their interests, without losing it in the endless flow of the feed.

6. Facebook Search for Business Owners

For business owners and marketers, Facebook search can be a powerful tool to understand your audience and track competitors.

Tracking Competitors

- **Competitor Search**: You can use Facebook search to monitor what competitors are doing. Type their business name or key product terms to find relevant pages and posts, giving you insight into their strategies.

Discovering Audience Trends

- **Exploring Audience Preferences**: Use search to discover what type of content is popular among your audience. Track trending hashtags and topics related to your industry, and tailor your content to fit these trends.

Conclusion

Using Facebook's search bar effectively is crucial to navigating the platform, whether you're a casual user or a business professional. By utilizing filters, hashtags, advanced operators, and the saved content feature, you can find specific people, pages, posts, and even market trends that matter most to you. Facebook's powerful search capabilities allow you to discover new opportunities, connect with like-minded people, and stay ahead in a world where social media is king.

8.3 Integrating Facebook with Other Apps

In the ever-evolving world of social media, Facebook is not only a platform for sharing updates, photos, and videos but also a central hub that connects with various other applications and services. Integrating Facebook with other apps can streamline your online experience, enhance your digital presence, and increase your efficiency. This chapter will explore how to connect Facebook with other popular apps, including Google, Instagram, and various third-party tools, and guide you through the benefits and practical steps of these integrations.

Why Integrate Facebook with Other Apps?

Before we dive into the specifics of integration, let's understand why you might want to integrate Facebook with other apps in the first place. Here are some of the main advantages:

1. **Cross-Platform Sharing**: By connecting Facebook with other apps, you can easily share content across multiple platforms without needing to upload it repeatedly. This saves you time and ensures your content reaches a broader audience.

2. **Increased Productivity**: Automating certain tasks, such as sharing posts or managing your content, frees up time for other important activities. Integrations help simplify many repetitive actions, allowing you to focus on content creation and engagement.

3. **Centralized Management**: By integrating Facebook with other apps, you can manage your social media accounts, communications, and marketing efforts all from a single interface. This is especially beneficial for business owners and marketers.

4. **Enhanced Analytics and Insights**: Integration with third-party apps, like analytics tools, provides deeper insights into your performance on Facebook, helping you optimize your strategy and improve engagement.

Popular Facebook Integrations

Now that we know the benefits, let's dive into some popular apps you can integrate with Facebook to enhance your experience. We'll cover both native Facebook integrations and third-party integrations.

1. Integrating Facebook with Instagram

Facebook and Instagram are both owned by Meta, which makes integrating the two platforms fairly simple. Many users and businesses find it highly effective to manage both platforms from a single interface.

How to Integrate Facebook with Instagram

1. **Connect Your Instagram Account to Facebook**:

   o Open the **Instagram app** and go to your **Profile**.

   o Tap the **three lines** in the top right corner and select **Settings**.

   o Scroll down and tap **Account**, then select **Linked Accounts**.

   o Choose **Facebook** and log in to your Facebook account to connect the two platforms.

2. **Linking Your Facebook Page to Instagram**:

   o If you manage a business account on Instagram, link it to your Facebook business page. This allows you to run ads across both platforms and share Instagram content directly to Facebook.

   o On Instagram, go to your business profile and tap **Edit Profile**.

   o Under **Public Business Information**, tap **Page**, then select your Facebook Page.

Benefits of Integration

- **Shared Posts**: You can share Instagram posts directly to Facebook, saving time and increasing the visibility of your content.

- **Cross-Platform Ads**: Run Instagram and Facebook ads from one place using Facebook's **Ad Manager**, increasing your reach and targeting potential customers effectively.

- **Instagram Insights on Facebook**: Access Instagram's analytics through your Facebook Page Insights, which helps you understand engagement metrics across both platforms.

2. Connecting Facebook with Google Tools (Google Drive, Google Photos, etc.)

Integrating Facebook with Google's suite of apps can significantly improve how you manage your media and content. From Google Photos to Google Drive, here's how you can connect your Facebook account with Google services.

How to Integrate Facebook with Google

1. **Linking Facebook to Google Photos**:
   - While there is no direct Facebook-to-Google Photos integration, you can download your photos from Facebook and upload them to Google Photos manually. You can also use tools like **Zapier** to create automated workflows that sync Facebook photos to Google Photos.

2. **Using Google Drive for Facebook Content Management**:
   - For businesses and marketers, organizing your Facebook content in Google Drive is a simple yet effective way to keep track of your media and other digital assets.
   - Download your content from Facebook (such as photos or videos) and upload it to **Google Drive** for easy access and management. You can also share these files with others for collaboration.

Benefits of Integration

- **Backup and Storage**: Keep a backup of your important Facebook content in Google Drive, ensuring you have a secure and organized storage solution.

- **Easy Sharing**: Google Drive allows you to easily share files with others, which can be useful if you're collaborating on content creation or need to share Facebook content for external projects.

- **Automating Content Posting**: Tools like Zapier can be used to automatically post new content from your Google Drive to Facebook.

3. Using Third-Party Tools for Facebook Management

Several third-party tools can help you integrate Facebook with other apps, manage your social media presence, and track performance. Let's explore some popular options:

Hootsuite

Hootsuite is a popular social media management tool that allows you to connect Facebook and other social networks to schedule posts, monitor conversations, and analyze performance.

1. **How to Connect Facebook to Hootsuite**:

    o Sign up for a Hootsuite account and connect your Facebook account by selecting **Add Social Network**.

    o Choose **Facebook** and follow the prompts to log into your Facebook account and grant permissions.

2. **Scheduling and Managing Posts**:

    o Once your accounts are connected, you can create and schedule Facebook posts for specific times. Hootsuite also allows you to manage multiple Facebook Pages and Groups from one dashboard.

Zapier

Zapier is an automation tool that connects Facebook with hundreds of other apps, such as Google Sheets, Slack, and Trello.

1. **How to Create a Facebook-Zapier Integration**:

    o Sign up for a Zapier account and connect your Facebook account to the app you wish to automate.

    o Choose a **Trigger** (e.g., "New Post on Facebook") and an **Action** (e.g., "Add Row in Google Sheets") to create your automation.

2. **Setting Up Automation**:

    o For example, you can set up a Zap that automatically logs all your Facebook posts in a Google Sheet, or one that sends a notification to your Slack channel whenever a new comment is made on your Facebook Page.

Buffer

Buffer is another powerful tool for managing your Facebook content. It allows for scheduling posts, analyzing engagement, and tracking content performance.

1. **How to Connect Facebook to Buffer**:

    o Connect your Facebook account to Buffer by selecting **Connect a Social Account** and logging into Facebook.

    o Buffer will then give you the ability to manage and schedule posts across multiple Facebook Pages.

2. **Buffer for Facebook Ads**:

    o Buffer's advanced features allow you to create Facebook ad campaigns directly from the platform and analyze their performance in real-time.

Canva for Facebook Content Creation

Canva is a popular tool for creating visually appealing content, such as Facebook cover photos, posts, and ads. Integrating Canva with Facebook can help streamline your design process.

1. **How to Use Canva with Facebook**:

    o After creating a design in Canva, you can directly publish it to your Facebook Page or use Canva's scheduling tool to set a specific time for posting.

2. **Facebook Ad Creation**:

    o Canva offers pre-made templates for Facebook Ads, making it easy to create eye-catching ads without needing graphic design experience.

Best Practices for Integrating Facebook with Other Apps

While integrating Facebook with other apps can be a game-changer, it's important to follow some best practices to ensure your experience is smooth and secure:

1. **Stay Secure**: Always review app permissions before connecting Facebook with any third-party app. Make sure you only grant necessary permissions and avoid sharing sensitive information.

2. **Automate Responsibly**: While automation tools like Zapier and Hootsuite can save you time, be careful not to over-automate. It's crucial to maintain an authentic and personal touch in your interactions with your audience.

3. **Regularly Review Integrations**: Technology and social media platforms are constantly evolving. Regularly review your integrations to ensure they are working as expected and providing value.

4. **Engage Consistently**: Automation and integrations can help with posting and managing content, but engagement is key. Always take the time to respond to comments, messages, and feedback from your audience.

Conclusion

Integrating Facebook with other apps opens up a wide range of possibilities for enhancing your social media experience. Whether you're managing personal profiles, running a business, or creating content for multiple platforms, these integrations will make your workflow more efficient and effective. By understanding and implementing the integrations we've covered in this chapter, you can unlock the full power of social media, saving time and increasing engagement across all your digital channels.

Conclusion

9.1 Recap of Key Learnings

In this section, we will revisit the core concepts and strategies you have learned throughout the book. This recap will help you reinforce key takeaways and provide a clear understanding of how to apply the lessons covered in each chapter to maximize your experience and effectiveness on Facebook.

Getting Started with Facebook

In the beginning, we explored the essentials of getting started on Facebook. Whether you are using Facebook for personal connections, business growth, or community engagement, your first steps on the platform are crucial.

1. **Creating an Account**: You learned how to create your own Facebook account and customize your profile. From choosing a profile and cover photo to adding personal details, we ensured you understood the importance of a complete profile that represents you authentically.

2. **Navigating the Facebook Interface**: The user interface on Facebook can be overwhelming at first, but understanding the layout and menu options allows you to easily find and manage the content that matters most. From the News Feed to the navigation bar, these components are all designed to give you quick access to your updates and friends.

3. **Security Basics**: A key aspect of your account setup involved understanding privacy settings and security measures, like setting up two-factor authentication. Protecting your account from unauthorized access was a primary focus, ensuring that you can enjoy a secure Facebook experience.

Building Your Network

One of Facebook's greatest strengths is its ability to connect people. In this section, we covered how to grow your online presence and build a community.

1. **Adding Friends and Followers**: Adding people you know and following pages that interest you are the starting points for building a network. You learned how to search for people, send friend requests, and manage your list of friends. We also touched on how to follow influential figures and pages that align with your interests or business.

2. **Joining Groups**: Groups are an excellent way to connect with like-minded individuals or potential customers. By joining or creating groups based on shared interests, hobbies, or business goals, you can establish a space for active engagement and networking. You learned the process of searching for relevant groups and how to participate meaningfully.

3. **Engaging with Communities**: Facebook is all about engagement, whether it's liking, commenting, sharing posts, or simply observing others' interactions. This section helped you develop a strategic approach to engagement, ensuring you are making meaningful connections rather than passively browsing.

Sharing Content on Facebook

Creating and sharing content on Facebook is where you can express yourself, build your personal or business brand, and engage with others.

1. **Posting Content**: You learned how to create posts that resonate with your audience. From simple status updates to sharing videos, photos, and articles, content creation is essential. This chapter explored the various types of posts you can make, along with tips on how to make them engaging.

2. **Stories and Reels**: We explored Facebook's more temporary forms of content—Stories and Reels. Both features allow you to share snippets of your day or create engaging, short-form content that disappears after 24 hours. Understanding how to create dynamic Stories and Reels is key to staying relevant and maintaining engagement.

3. **Managing Your Content**:After posting, the next step is managing your content. This involves editing or deleting posts and monitoring who can view your content. Ensuring that your content is shared with the appropriate audience helps protect your privacy and ensures you are maintaining control over what is seen.

Mastering Facebook Features

Facebook is much more than just a social platform; it includes an array of features that can enhance your experience and extend your reach.

1. **Messenger**:
    One of the most powerful features of Facebook is its integrated messaging system, Messenger. You learned how to send text, voice, and video messages to friends and businesses. Messenger allows you to stay in constant communication and even conduct business.

2. **Facebook Events**: Facebook events make it easy to organize both virtual and in-person gatherings. You discovered how to create and manage events, invite attendees, and track RSVPs. This feature is invaluable for both personal social gatherings and business-related events.

3. **Marketplace**:
    For those looking to buy or sell items locally, Facebook Marketplace is an incredibly useful tool. We discussed how to post your own listings, browse for products, and communicate with buyers and sellers. Facebook Marketplace helps you reach a wide audience with minimal effort.

Growing Your Presence on Facebook

Building a strong presence on Facebook goes beyond just having an account—it requires strategic growth and consistent efforts.

1. **Personal Branding**: One of the main reasons people use Facebook is to build their personal or business brand. Whether you are an entrepreneur, influencer, or just someone who wants to enhance their online identity, we outlined methods for effectively presenting yourself. From posting value-driven content to actively engaging with your followers, you now know how to grow your brand.

2. **Facebook for Business**: Facebook is a valuable marketing tool for businesses of all sizes. You learned how to create a Facebook business page, how to engage with followers, and the importance of Facebook Insights for tracking performance. Running a business on Facebook means providing relevant, helpful content while interacting with potential customers.

3. **Running Facebook Ads**: Facebook Ads are one of the most effective ways to reach a targeted audience. You learned how to set up an ad campaign, target specific demographics, and track your ad's performance using Facebook's powerful advertising tools. This section helped you understand the full potential of Facebook's advertising platform.

Managing Your Privacy and Security

Maintaining your privacy and security on Facebook is essential in today's digital world.

1. **Privacy Settings**: Throughout the book, we've highlighted the importance of securing your account and protecting your personal data. From adjusting who can see your posts to reviewing Facebook's privacy checkups, you have learned how to ensure your profile is as private as you want it to be.

2. **Protecting Your Data**: Understanding how to download a copy of your data and how to deactivate or delete your account gives you complete control over your information. These actions ensure that you can safeguard your data and take necessary actions if your account is compromised.

3. **Avoiding Scams and Fake Profiles**: Facebook is full of both genuine users and fraudulent accounts. Recognizing and reporting fake profiles, as well as knowing how to stay safe online, ensures that you don't fall victim to scams. We've equipped you with the knowledge to identify and report suspicious activity.

Advanced Facebook Tips and Tricks

In the final chapters, we covered advanced strategies to help you make the most of Facebook.

1. **Optimizing Your Profile for Networking**: A well-optimized profile can make a huge difference in the way people perceive you on Facebook. You learned how to optimize your bio, use keywords strategically, and build a profile that enhances your professional network.

2. **Using Facebook Search Like a Pro**: Facebook's search function is a powerful tool, allowing you to find people, groups, and content with ease. You now know how to use filters and search operators to get more relevant results quickly.

3. **Integrating Facebook with Other Apps**: Facebook seamlessly integrates with other applications, which can make your social media experience more efficient. Whether it's using Facebook with Instagram, WhatsApp, or external apps, this integration can increase productivity and engagement.

Conclusion

As we conclude this book, we hope that you now feel confident in your ability to navigate, use, and maximize Facebook to your advantage. By following the steps and strategies outlined throughout this guide, you've unlocked the potential of one of the most influential social media platforms in the world.

Remember that Facebook is constantly evolving, and the key to success is staying up-to-date and continuing to engage in meaningful ways. Whether for personal connections, business marketing, or community involvement, Facebook offers limitless possibilities for those who know how to use it well.

9.2 Future Trends on Facebook

Facebook, as one of the most influential social media platforms globally, is constantly evolving to meet the needs of its users and advertisers. As we look into the future, several key trends are likely to shape the way people interact with the platform, the way businesses engage with their audiences, and the overall impact of Facebook on society. This section will explore these trends in depth, providing insight into what Facebook users can expect in the coming years.

1. The Continued Rise of Video Content

Over the last few years, video content has seen tremendous growth on Facebook, with both short-form and long-form videos becoming a central part of the user experience. Facebook has been prioritizing video in the News Feed, especially videos that are more engaging and interactive.

Why This Trend Matters:

- Facebook's algorithm now rewards video content more than static posts, meaning videos are more likely to be shown to your audience. Whether you're a business or a personal brand, incorporating video into your content strategy is becoming essential.

- Facebook Live, which allows users to broadcast live video, has become a critical tool for engagement. As technology improves, the quality of live broadcasts will continue to rise, and features like live shopping and virtual events will make it even more interactive.

- Short-form video platforms like Instagram Reels have proven successful and are being increasingly integrated with Facebook. Expect to see more cross-platform video sharing and new tools to make video content even more user-friendly.

What the Future Holds:

- **Advanced Video Editing Tools**: Facebook will likely provide more advanced video editing options, enabling users to create professional-level videos directly on the platform. Expect easier integrations with augmented reality (AR) and virtual reality (VR) for more immersive experiences.

- **360-Degree and 3D Videos**: With the ongoing development of virtual reality, Facebook might heavily invest in 360-degree and 3D videos, offering users more interactive ways to consume content.

- **More Live Streaming Opportunities**: Live streaming will not only grow for casual users but will also be a critical business tool. Expect more tools and features to enhance interactivity during live streams, such as live Q&A, polls, and direct purchasing features.

2. The Integration of Augmented Reality (AR) and Virtual Reality (VR)

Facebook's parent company, Meta, has been heavily investing in AR and VR technologies, and these innovations will start to play a more prominent role on the Facebook platform. The metaverse, a virtual space where people can socialize, work, and create, is at the core of this transition.

Why This Trend Matters:

- Augmented Reality and Virtual Reality technologies have already begun transforming the way users engage with content. Features like AR filters in Facebook Stories are just the beginning.

- Meta's development of the Oculus VR headset positions Facebook to provide more immersive, virtual social experiences, where users can attend virtual events, hang out with friends in a virtual space, and experience 3D environments.

What the Future Holds:

- **More AR Filters and Effects**: As AR technology becomes more accessible and integrated into Facebook's ecosystem, we can expect a wider variety of AR filters and effects available for both casual and business users.

- **Social VR Spaces**: Facebook could offer entirely new ways to interact within virtual spaces. You could soon be able to "meet" friends or coworkers in a virtual room, collaborate on projects, or attend live concerts or conferences in VR.

- **E-commerce and AR Shopping**: AR technology will likely become a key part of Facebook's e-commerce offering. Expect users to virtually try on clothes, test products in their own environment, or even attend VR shopping events.

3. Enhanced E-Commerce and Social Shopping

Facebook has been positioning itself as a leader in social commerce, allowing businesses to sell directly to users through Marketplace, Shops, and advertising. The future of shopping on Facebook will likely see deeper integrations with other platforms, offering seamless shopping experiences.

Why This Trend Matters:

- Facebook is increasingly becoming a place not just for social interaction but for buying and selling. Facebook Shops and Instagram Shops make it easier for small businesses to reach global customers directly from their pages.

- The social aspect of shopping is growing. Product reviews, influencer endorsements, and peer recommendations will continue to influence purchasing decisions on Facebook.

What the Future Holds:

- **Seamless Shopping Experience**: Expect further integrations between Facebook Shops and the wider e-commerce world. Businesses will be able to connect their inventory directly with Facebook's platform for smoother transactions.

- **Increased Use of AI for Personalized Recommendations**: Facebook's algorithm will continue to improve, providing more personalized shopping experiences based on user data. This could mean more accurate product suggestions, better targeting for advertisements, and personalized promotions.

- **Live Shopping and Virtual Try-Ons**: Live shopping events, where users can purchase products directly during live broadcasts, will become more common. Brands may also implement AR technology to allow users to virtually try on products before making a purchase.

4. Further Focus on Privacy and Data Security

Given the scrutiny Facebook has faced regarding privacy concerns, the platform is expected to continue making improvements in this area to rebuild trust with users.

Why This Trend Matters:

- Privacy and data security are becoming major concerns for users of all social media platforms, not just Facebook. Facebook has made some adjustments to improve transparency and user control over data, but much work remains to be done.

- Facebook will need to stay ahead of the curve to maintain user confidence and avoid regulatory challenges that could negatively impact its growth.

What the Future Holds:

- **More Transparent Privacy Controls**: Facebook will likely make privacy controls easier to understand, giving users more direct control over how their data is used and shared.

- **Better Data Encryption**: Expect more robust data encryption to ensure that sensitive user information remains private and secure.

- **Compliance with New Regulations**: As data privacy laws evolve (such as the GDPR in Europe), Facebook will need to ensure compliance with various national and international regulations. This could lead to changes in how data is stored and shared.

5. Artificial Intelligence (AI) and Machine Learning Innovations

Facebook is already using AI in its platform to improve user experience, and this trend will accelerate in the future. From advanced algorithms that personalize your News Feed to AI-powered chatbots for businesses, Facebook is heavily investing in artificial intelligence.

Why This Trend Matters:

- AI can enhance user experience by providing more relevant content, improving search results, and offering smarter ad targeting.

- For businesses, AI tools could automate customer service, track ad performance, and optimize campaigns.

What the Future Holds:

- **Smarter Content Curation**: The use of AI to curate and recommend content will become even more sophisticated. Facebook will better understand your preferences and show you content that is most likely to engage you.

- **AI-Powered Chatbots**: Businesses will be able to deploy more advanced AI-driven chatbots that provide instant, personalized responses to customer inquiries, improving the overall customer experience.

- **Automated Content Moderation**: AI will play a critical role in detecting harmful content, fake news, and hate speech, helping to maintain a safer online environment.

6. Integration with Messaging Apps and Cross-Platform Communication

As communication on Facebook continues to evolve, integration with Facebook Messenger and other platforms will become more seamless.

Why This Trend Matters:

- Facebook Messenger already serves as a robust messaging platform, and its integration with Facebook itself is a major advantage for users who want to stay connected across different platforms.

- As communication increasingly moves to digital platforms, users will demand more integrated experiences.

What the Future Holds:

- **Cross-Platform Messaging**: Expect to see even more integration between Facebook Messenger, Instagram Direct, and WhatsApp, making it easier for users to manage conversations from multiple apps in one place.

- **Business and Consumer Interaction via Messenger**: More businesses will offer customer support, booking services, and sales directly through Messenger, leading to a richer, more interactive customer service experience.

Conclusion:

Facebook's future is undoubtedly intertwined with emerging technologies such as AI, AR/VR, and advanced data security. The platform is evolving to offer a more immersive, personalized, and secure experience for users and businesses alike. As Facebook continues to innovate and adapt, the platform will remain an essential tool for communication, socialization, and commerce in the coming years.

These trends provide a glimpse of what users and businesses can expect on Facebook. By staying up to date with these developments, individuals can make the most of their Facebook presence, whether for personal use or business growth.

9.3 Final Tips for Facebook Success

In the fast-paced world of social media, Facebook remains one of the most powerful platforms for personal and professional growth. With over 2.8 billion active users worldwide, Facebook offers an unparalleled opportunity for individuals, businesses, and organizations to connect, engage, and thrive. However, to fully unlock the potential of Facebook, it's important to not only understand the basics of the platform but also implement strategies and best practices that can help you stand out, stay secure, and build meaningful relationships. This section will cover final tips for Facebook success, ensuring that you can maximize your impact and make the most of your time on the platform.

1. Build a Strong Personal Brand

One of the most important things to keep in mind when using Facebook is the concept of personal branding. Your profile is essentially an online representation of who you are, and how you present yourself on the platform can make a significant impact on your personal and professional reputation.

Define Your Purpose Before posting anything on Facebook, take a moment to consider why you're using the platform in the first place. Are you looking to connect with friends and family, network with industry professionals, promote a business, or simply share content for entertainment? Defining your purpose will guide the way you interact with Facebook and ensure that you remain focused on your goals.

Be Consistent Whether you're sharing posts, commenting, or engaging with others, consistency is key. This doesn't mean you need to post every day, but establishing a routine or a consistent posting schedule can help keep you relevant. When it comes to creating content, make sure it aligns with your personal brand and speaks to your audience in a way that resonates with them.

Stay Authentic People connect with authenticity. While it's important to stay professional, especially in a business context, don't be afraid to show your personality. Share behind-the-scenes glimpses of your life, let your sense of humor shine through, and engage with others in a genuine way. Authenticity will help you build trust and create stronger relationships with your network.

2. Create and Share Valuable Content

Content is the heart of Facebook. Whether you're posting personal updates, sharing articles, or promoting products, what you share has the power to engage your audience and encourage interaction. However, the content you post should not only be relevant but also valuable to your audience.

Know Your Audience To create content that resonates, you need to understand your audience's preferences, interests, and needs. Take the time to analyze your friends, followers, and page visitors to gain insight into what they care about. Use Facebook Insights (for business pages) to track engagement and identify the types of content that perform best.

Offer Value, Not Just Promotion While it's okay to promote your business, service, or personal achievements, be sure to offer value beyond just promotional content. Share useful tips, inspirational quotes, entertaining stories, and industry news. Educating your audience or providing them with insightful content will keep them engaged and encourage them to return for more.

Visual Content Works Best Posts with images, videos, and infographics tend to perform better than text-only updates. Visual content captures attention and is more likely to be shared. If you want to make an impact, invest in high-quality visuals that align with your message and resonate with your audience.

3. Engage with Your Audience

Engagement is a critical element of Facebook success. The more you engage with your audience, the more likely they are to engage back, creating a cycle of interaction that can amplify your presence.

Respond to Comments and Messages Promptly When someone takes the time to comment on your post or message you directly, it's important to respond in a timely and thoughtful manner. This shows that you value their input and creates a sense of community around your profile. Prompt responses also increase the likelihood that your posts will be seen by more people, as Facebook's algorithm tends to favor posts with higher engagement.

Ask Questions Encourage your audience to engage with your posts by asking questions. Simple prompts like "What do you think?" or "Have you experienced this too?" can lead to valuable conversations. Asking questions also signals to Facebook's algorithm that your post is sparking interest, which can help increase its reach.

Participate in Discussions Don't just post content—actively participate in discussions, comment on other people's posts, and engage with groups. By contributing to conversations, you establish yourself as an active member of the Facebook community, which helps you build relationships and increase your visibility.

4. Take Advantage of Facebook Groups

Facebook Groups are one of the best tools for building a tight-knit community around a shared interest, profession, or cause. Whether you want to connect with like-minded individuals or grow a business, Facebook Groups offer an excellent platform for engagement and relationship-building.

Join Relevant Groups Look for groups that align with your interests, whether they are related to your industry, hobbies, or personal passions. Joining relevant groups allows you to learn from others, share your expertise, and stay updated on the latest trends and discussions in your field.

Create Your Own Group If you can't find a group that suits your needs, consider creating your own. By creating a group, you position yourself as a leader in your niche, which can help you build a community of people who share your interests and values. Make sure to set clear guidelines for participation to ensure that the group remains positive, valuable, and welcoming.

Engage Actively in Groups Be active within the groups you're a part of. Offer advice, answer questions, share relevant content, and build relationships with other members. The more you engage, the more you will be recognized as an expert and go-to person within the group.

5. Optimize Your Facebook Ads

If you're looking to grow your brand or business on Facebook, investing in Facebook Ads is one of the most effective ways to do so. Facebook Ads provide you with the ability to target specific demographics, track performance, and increase visibility.

Know Your Audience Before launching any ad campaign, make sure you have a clear understanding of who your target audience is. Use Facebook's targeting features to define your audience based on factors like age, location, interests, and behaviors. The more precise your targeting, the more effective your ads will be.

Test Different Ad Formats Facebook offers a variety of ad formats, including photo ads, video ads, carousel ads, and more. Experiment with different types of ads to see which one performs best for your goals. Running A/B tests will help you identify the most effective strategies for reaching your audience.

Monitor and Optimize Your Ads Once your ads are live, monitor their performance using Facebook Ads Manager. Track metrics such as engagement, clicks, and conversions. Based on this data, optimize your ads by adjusting targeting, ad copy, visuals, and budgets to improve results.

6. Stay Up-to-Date with Facebook's Evolving Features

Facebook is constantly evolving, and it's important to stay up-to-date with its new features and updates. Regularly check Facebook's official blog and updates section to learn about new tools and changes to existing ones.

Experiment with New Features When Facebook rolls out new features, take the time to experiment with them and see how they can benefit your social media strategy. Whether it's a new type of post, a revamped ad format, or an updated privacy feature, trying new things will help you stay ahead of the curve.

Learn from Others Follow industry leaders, successful marketers, and social media influencers to learn how they're using Facebook to build their brands. Join webinars, attend virtual conferences, and participate in Facebook communities that focus on social media strategies to keep learning and improving.

7. Prioritize Your Security and Privacy

The final piece of advice for Facebook success is ensuring that you protect your account and data. In the digital age, cybersecurity is more important than ever, and taking steps to secure your Facebook account is crucial.

Review Your Privacy Settings Regularly Facebook allows you to control who can see your posts, send you friend requests, and message you. Regularly review your privacy settings to ensure that you're comfortable with who can access your information. Set your posts to "Friends Only" if you want to limit visibility and adjust your profile settings to ensure that only trusted individuals can contact you.

Be Mindful of What You Share While Facebook can be a great platform for sharing personal experiences, be mindful of the information you disclose. Avoid sharing sensitive personal data such as your home address or financial information. Remember that once something is posted online, it can be difficult to completely erase.

Report Suspicious Activity If you encounter fake profiles, suspicious messages, or content that violates Facebook's community standards, report it. Facebook takes security seriously, and reporting harmful activity helps keep the platform safe for everyone.

By following these final tips, you'll be well on your way to mastering Facebook and unlocking the true power of this incredible platform. Whether you're using it for personal connections, networking, business growth, or creative expression, Facebook offers endless possibilities to engage with the world around you. Stay authentic, continue learning, and always prioritize your security and privacy as you navigate the social media landscape.

Acknowledgements

First and foremost, I would like to extend my heartfelt gratitude to you, the reader, for choosing to invest your time and energy into this book. Whether you picked it up to enhance your personal social media skills, learn new strategies for business growth, or simply explore the world of Facebook, your support means the world to me.

Creating this guide has been an exciting and fulfilling journey, and I hope that the tips, insights, and strategies shared here have empowered you to navigate Facebook with confidence, whether for personal use or professional success. I truly believe that the power of social media lies in how we choose to harness it, and I hope this book has provided you with the tools to make the most of what Facebook has to offer.

A special thank you goes out to all of those who helped make this book a reality. To my family and friends for their unwavering encouragement and patience, to my editors for their insightful feedback, and to my readers for their enthusiasm and support throughout the process — I am forever grateful.

Lastly, I want to encourage you to continue exploring, learning, and growing on Facebook. Social media is constantly evolving, and as you implement the tips and strategies from this book, I am confident that you'll be able to unlock even more opportunities in your personal and professional life.

Thank you again for your trust in this guide. I wish you great success as you navigate the dynamic world of Facebook!

Warm regards,